FOR
ALL
TIME

Doxology!

Exploring and enjoying
the New Testament benedictions

Stan K Evers

DayOne

© Day One Publications 2012
First printed 2012

ISBN 978–1–84625–311–9

British Library Cataloguing in Publication Data available

Published by Day One Publications
Ryelands Road, Leominster, HR6 8NZ
☎ 01568 613 740 FAX 01568 611 473
email—sales@dayone.co.uk
web site—www.dayone.co.uk
North America—email—usasales@dayone.co.uk

Cover design by Wayne McMaster
Printed by Orchard Press Cheltenham Ltd

The following pages are dedicated to Revd. John Potter,
who baptized me, when I was fourteen,
at Tollington Park Baptist Church, London,
on 9 July 1961.

Thank you, Mr Mike Boland, for checking the text and for your
encouragement.

Appreciations

The benedictions and doxologies of the New Testament—what a good idea for a book, and what a good book! With clarity and perception, Stan Evers takes us through these passages that are often neglected, consistently pointing us to the greatness and glory of our sovereign God and calling us to praise. If there is a lack of praise in your life, read this book. You will be blessed.

Roger Ellsworth, Pastor, Parkview Baptist Church, Jackson, TN, USA

This helpful little book is clearly the result of a lot of hard work and study, and Christian people should be grateful to Stan Evers for taking the time to elucidate these important but sometimes neglected New Testament passages, some familiar and some less so. By God's grace, what Stan has to say will make us long for heaven, where, as he says, one day 'we will sing for ever with sinless souls and glorified bodies' in such terms.

Gary Brady, Pastor, Child's Hill Baptist Church, London, UK

While many Christians would think only of two or three benedictions to end a service of worship, Stan Evers has collected twenty-eight of them, only looking at the New Testament, and there are also huge numbers in the Old Testament. Using very clear, straightforward language, the author leads us into helpful meditations on each of these, applying their truths to our everyday lives. This book will stimulate many to stop and think about these powerful words of Scripture.

Michael Bentley, retired pastor, Bracknell, UK

Contents

Contents

Let us begin with two simple definitions: a benediction is a prayer and a doxology is praise. Of course, benedictions are sometimes praise and a doxology is often a prayer. However, I would suggest that prayer is more prominent in benediction and praise is more prominent in doxology. The two often overlap in the New Testament— for example, in Jude 24–25 and Ephesians 3:20–21.

The word 'benediction' comes from two Latin words that mean 'to speak well of'; 'doxology' is derived from the Greek word for 'glory'. At the close of worship many congregations regularly listen to, or say together, a benediction, and may even sing a doxology, as they seek God's favour for the future and praise him for his favour in the past.

Several benedictions seek the blessing of, and render praise to, the triune God: God the Father, God the Son and God the Holy Spirit. An example is the benediction of 2 Corinthians 13:14: 'May the grace of the Lord Jesus Christ, and the love of God, and the fellowship of the Holy Spirit be with you all.'

The Bible overflows with benedictions, yet preachers and others leading worship probably use only three or four of these, such as Numbers 6:24–26; 2 Corinthians 13:14; Ephesians 3:20–21; and Jude 24–25. The benediction selected often does not appear to have any connection with the sermon that has just been preached. It could be argued that as the hymns, apart from the closing one, do not necessarily link to the sermon, the benediction does not need to either. We are seeking God's blessing rather than reiterating the sermon. But perhaps this overuse of a few benedictions means that congregations do not pay much attention to them; a benediction is merely the signal that the service has finished.

My reading on this subject suggests that churches with a liturgical structure of worship have treated benedictions—biblical and non-biblical—more seriously than other worshippers. Does this reflect a reaction, especially in Nonconformist churches, against the unscriptural idea that the minister has sacerdotal powers to convey the blessings pronounced in the benediction?

Paul's benedictions and doxologies are from time to time preceded by what we might call a 'preface'. A case in point is the doxology of Galatians 1:5, 'to whom be glory for ever and ever'. The 'preface' that begins in verse 3 is essential to the doxology of verse 5 and provides the reason why we ought to praise 'our God and Father' (v. 4): because of the Saviour's substitutionary death as part of God's eternal plan to save his people. Another example is the benediction in 1 Corinthians 16:23–24, which is preceded by Paul's greetings and the 'curse' on all who do not love Christ (vv. 19–22). The context adds to our understanding of the two final verses of the chapter.

I have restricted this book to New Testament benedictions and doxologies so that it does not become too long! Yet there are so many rich and wonderful benedictions and doxologies in the Old Testament, especially in the book of Psalms: for instance, Psalms 20 and 41. The most famous, and most often used, is Aaron's benediction of Numbers 6:24–26: 'The LORD bless you and keep you; the LORD make his face shine upon you and be gracious to you; the LORD turn his face towards you and give you peace.'

A study of the New Testament benedictions and doxologies has deepened my own worship of the triune God. I pray that it will also enrich your worship. May these benedictions and doxologies make us long for heaven, where we will sing for ever, with sinless souls and glorified bodies,

'Worthy is the Lamb, who was slain,
to receive power and wealth and strength
and honour and glory and praise! …'
'To him who sits on the throne and to the Lamb
be praise and honour and glory and power
for ever and ever!' (Rev. 5:12–13)

The angels' song (Luke 2:13–14)

Suddenly a great company of the heavenly host appeared with the angel, praising God and saying, 'Glory to God in the highest, and on earth peace to men on whom his favour rests.'

This doxology is one of five songs in the opening two chapters of the Gospel of Luke. We listen to the songs of Elizabeth (1:42–45), Mary (1:46–55), Zechariah (1:68–79), the angels (2:14) and Simeon (2:29–32). Three of these songs are on the lips of old Jewish believers: Elizabeth, Zechariah and Simeon; one song is that of a young pregnant virgin, Mary. The remaining song is unique because it is the chorus of 'a great company of the heavenly host'. All five songs celebrate the birth of Jesus, the promised Messiah.

Five songs

Elizabeth's song is a benediction—notice the word 'blessed' (1:42, 45)—in which she praises God for Mary's privilege of being 'the mother of my Lord' (v. 43). Mary's song, now known as 'The Magnificat' ('My soul doth magnify the Lord', 1:46, KJV), is a doxology in which she praises God, who is mighty (vv. 49, 51), majestic ('holy is his name', v. 49) and merciful (vv. 50, 54).

Pause for a moment to think of the cost to Mary in becoming the virgin mother of Jesus.

It was no light matter to become the mother of our Lord in this unheard and mysterious way. It brought with it, no doubt, at a distant period great honour; but it brought with it for the present no small danger and trial to Mary's faith. All this danger and trial the holy Virgin was willing and ready to risk. She asks no further questions. She raises no further objections. She accepts the honour laid upon her, with all its attendant perils and inconveniences.[1]

Zechariah's song is a benediction ('Blessed be the Lord', 1:68, KJV) that takes the form of a prophecy (1:67). He predicts that his son, later known as John the Baptist, will be 'called a prophet of the Most High' (v. 76) and that through Mary's Son many will know God and receive the forgiveness of sins (v. 77). The Saviour's birth reveals 'the tender mercy of our God' (v. 78).

The word 'tender' (v. 78) translates the Greek word *splagchnon*, which was used to refer to internal organs, specifically the bowels or intestines (hence the KJV translation of Philippians 1:8 as 'the bowels of Jesus Christ'). In other places in the Bible (e.g. Col. 3:12; Philem. 7.12, 20) the apostle Paul uses the word to mean selfless and compassionate love. Zechariah's phrase 'the tender mercy of our God' means that God expressed his deep love for sinners by sending his own Son into the world in order to die a painful death on a cross.

Simeon's song—the fifth in the sequence—is a doxology addressed to the 'Sovereign Lord' (Luke 2:29) and identifies 'the child Jesus' as the Saviour promised by God (2:27, 29–30). This identification was confirmed by an old saint, Anna, who 'gave thanks to God and spoke about the child to all who were looking forward to the redemption of Jerusalem' (v. 38).

The careful reader will notice that Elizabeth 'exclaimed' (1:42), 'Mary said' (1:46), Zechariah 'prophesied' (1:67), the angels praised God, 'saying' (2:13) and Simeon 'praised God, saying' (2:28)—none of them sang! Nevertheless, each song is 'a Greek reproduction of a Semitic piece of poetry', a 'metrical composition'.[2]

Before the song of aged Simeon, shepherds heard the song of angels. We now turn our attention to the shepherds and think about what they saw and heard.

The shepherds

The appearance of just one angel filled the shepherds with fear (2:9–10). The terror of these robust shepherds shows that angels are not like pretty little children dressed in white! Angels are glorious, mighty and holy.[3] This herald angel came from God's presence to proclaim Messiah's birth (vv. 11–12). Then 'a great company of the heavenly host appeared with the angel, praising God' (v. 13).

We ought to notice that God spoke to the shepherds in the fields, not to the king in the palace, nor to the religious leaders in the temple. The shepherds' work kept them away from the temple and the synagogue, besides making them ceremonially unclean. 'The birth of a King's son is generally made an occasion of public revelling and rejoicing. The announcement of the birth of the Prince of Peace was made privately, at midnight, and without anything of worldly pomp and ostentation.'[4]

The shepherds' response to the angel's message and the angels' doxology was to hurry to Bethlehem, where they found 'Mary and Joseph, and the baby, who was lying in the manger' (v. 16). They believed what God had said—this is faith! Having believed, 'they spread the word' (v. 17)—this is evangelism! Those who know the Saviour want to tell everyone about him!

The angel's message

Before the angels' song, one angel declared the time of Christ's birth—'today'—and pointed to the place of his birth—'the town of David' (v. 11), that is, Bethlehem, fulfilling the prophecy of Micah 5:2. This angel also described the circumstances of his birth: 'You will find a baby wrapped in cloths and lying in a manger' (v. 12).

The baby in the manger was 'A Saviour … [who] is Christ the Lord' (v. 11). The designation 'Saviour' is the meaning of his name Jesus, given to Mary by the angel Gabriel and given to Joseph by 'an angel of the Lord' (1:31; Matt. 1:20–21). Later, Paul emphatically declared, 'Christ Jesus came into the world to save sinners' (1 Tim. 1:15).

The infant was also the Christ of whom the prophets wrote and for whom the Jewish race waited. Christ means 'the Anointed One'. Jewish prophets, priests and kings were anointed with oil—a symbol of God's Spirit—when they began their work or ascended the throne. The Holy Spirit came on Jesus at his baptism when he was aged thirty, to anoint him as the Prophet, Priest and King (Luke 3:21–23; see also 4:1, 18–19; John 3:34; Heb. 9:14).

Christ is the eternal King—'the Lord' (Luke 2:11)—not of one nation, but of the entire universe. He is 'the Lamb' who is 'Lord of lords and King of kings', the One who never dies and can never be toppled from his throne; he will reign for ever (Rev. 17:14; 19:16)!

The angel told the shepherds that Jesus was 'a Saviour … born to you' (Luke 2:11). He was born to save all who, like the shepherds, believe God's message, which comes to us now not through angels, but in the Bible.

The angels' song

The angels extolled God's glory and God's grace—two motifs heard in all the New Testament benedictions and doxologies (Luke 2:14).

GOD'S GLORY

The angels sang, 'Glory to God in the highest.' Creation glorified God, but not as much as did the incarnation of his Son, the Lord Jesus Christ, for the purpose of dying on a cross to redeem sinners. Angels in heaven and people everywhere on earth should offer to the Most High God the highest praise.

GOD'S GRACE

The angels also sang, '... on earth peace to men on whom his favour rests'; or, in the familiar language of the KJV, often quoted but misunderstood, 'on earth peace, good will toward men'. The angels were not singing about being nice to everyone at Christmas; rather, they were declaring that sinners can be at peace with God because of his goodwill—his grace—towards us.

It is God's favour to sinners that was the emphasis of the angels' chorus. All believers, like Mary, are 'highly favoured' (Luke 1:28); we 'have found favour with God' (1:30), not because of our merit but because of his sovereign grace. Mary, a sinner like ourselves, 'rejoice[d] in God [her] Saviour' (1:47).

We are rebels against the holy God; he is angry with us because of our sin (Rom. 1:18; 5:10; 8:6–8).5 However, the offended God sent Christ, his own Son, to earth as the 'Prince of Peace' (Isa. 9:6). It is through him that we have peace with God (Rom. 5:1). God declared Christ guilty in our place; he treated him as if he were a sinner. God declares us 'not guilty'; he treats us as if we had never sinned. This is the doctrine of justification.

The apostle Paul wrote about God's goodwill—his favour towards sinners—in all his letters. Two examples suffice: 'He predestined us to be adopted as his sons through Jesus Christ, in accordance with his pleasure and will—to the praise of his glorious grace, which he has freely given us in the One he loves' (Eph. 1:5–6); 'when the kindness and love of God our Saviour appeared, he saved us, not because of righteous things we had done, but because of his mercy' (Titus 3:4–5).

God's undeserved grace is 'good news of great joy' for 'all the people' (Luke 2:10)—sinners, whatever their ethnic origins, social standing or educational abilities. To quote Paul, 'there is no difference between Jew and Gentile—the same Lord is Lord of all and richly blesses all who call on him, for, "Everyone who calls on the name of the Lord will be saved"' (Rom. 10:12–13; see also Joel 2:32).

Chapter 1

The gospel of grace was the theme of the angels' doxology. Angels have 'never known a fallen world like this', but thank God that we may approach God's awesome presence through the 'offering and … sacrifice' made by Christ who is our 'Advocate with God'.[6] As redeemed sinners, we have a deeper understanding of God's grace than the highest angel near God's throne!

Jesus taught that those who know God's favour will show favour to others; this is the evidence that they are his children: 'Our Father … Forgive us our debts [sins], as we also have forgiven our debtors … For if you forgive men when they sin against you, your heavenly Father will also forgive you. But if you do not forgive men their sins, your Father will not forgive your sins' (Matt. 6:9, 12, 14–15; see also 5:43–48). Paul exhorted the Roman believers to 'Live in harmony with one another … If it is possible, as far as it depends on you, live at peace with everyone' (Rom. 12:16, 18).

The Saviour lives

'We do not need to have angels announce the good news of Christmas to follow the example of the shepherds. We can, and must, rejoice, because the Saviour over whom the angels and shepherds rejoiced still lives and still saves. Now that is a cause for joy!'[7] The angels' song is not just for Christmas!

Notes

1 **J. C. Ryle,** *Expository Thoughts on the Gospels: St Luke,* vol. i (London: James Clarke, 1956), p. 20.
2 **William Hendriksen,** *Gospel of Luke* (New Testament Commentary; Edinburgh: Banner of Truth, 1978), p. 95.
3 See **Roger Ellsworth,** *What the Bible Teaches about Angels* (Darlington: Evangelical Press, 2005).
4 **Ryle,** *Expository Thoughts: St. Luke,* pp. 55–56.
5 For a clear, and brief, exposition of Romans, read **Stuart Olyott,** *The Gospel As It Really Is: Romans Simply Explained* (Welwyn Commentary; Welwyn: Evangelical Press, 1979).

6 **Thomas Binney,** 'Eternal Light!', 1826.

7 **Roger Ellsworth,** *The 31 Days of Christmas: A Book of Daily Readings* (Welwyn: Evangelical Press, 1999), p. 30.

'God over all'
(Rom. 9:5)

Theirs are the patriarchs, and from them is traced the human ancestry of Christ, who is God over all, for ever praised! Amen.

W hat debates this verse has fuelled! Theologians, especially those who want to undermine Christ's deity, argue about the order and punctuation of the verse, and some even claim that this statement is not a doxology at all. But however the verse is translated, it is clear that Paul places Christ on a par with God.[1]

Charles Hodge, nineteenth-century American theologian, sums up the view of Reformed evangelical scholars: 'Paul ... declares that Christ, who ... as to his human nature ... descended from the Israelites, is ... the supreme God, or God over all, and blessed for ever.'[2] In this one verse the apostle affirms that Christ has two natures: he is man, deriving his 'human ancestry' from birth within the Jewish race; he is also 'God over all'—the eternal, uncreated God the Son, the second Person of the divine Trinity. This Trinitarian motif runs through many of the biblical benedictions and doxologies.

Paul's mention of 'the human ancestry of Christ' looks back to the opening chapter of the letter to the Romans: 'the gospel of God ... regarding his Son, who as to his human nature was a descendant of David' (1:1, 3).

'God over all'
An essential rule for interpreting the Bible—the theological term is

hermeneutics—is to compare Scripture with Scripture. Are there other Scriptures in which the apostle calls Christ God? Yes, there are. Take, as an example, Paul's farewell to the Ephesian elders: 'Be shepherds of the church of God, which he bought with his own blood' (Acts 20:28). We may add to this the apostle's words to his assistant Titus: 'we wait for the blessed hope—the glorious appearing of our great God and Saviour, Jesus Christ' (Titus 2:13). In his letters to the Philippians and to the Colossians, Paul writes about God coming to earth as a man in a human body: '… Christ Jesus: Who being in very nature God … being made in human likeness …'; 'in Christ all the fullness of the Deity lives in bodily form' (Phil. 2:5–7; Col. 2:9).

Where is Jesus Christ now? God

raised him from the dead and seated him at his right hand in the heavenly realms, far above all rule and authority, power and dominion, and every title that can be given, not only in this present age but also in the one to come. And God placed all things under his feet and appointed him to be head over everything for the church, which is his body, the fullness of him who fills everything in every way. (Eph. 1:20–23)

The power which raised Christ from the dead works in the souls of believers (Eph. 1:18–19).

The expression 'God over all' is used in Ephesians 4:6: 'one God and Father of all, who is over all and through all and in all'. The repetition of 'all' indicates that the apostle's theme in that chapter is the unity of the church, the body of Christ.

Divine and human

The Gospel writers give us an insight into the mysterious interplay of Christ's divine and human natures in several of Jesus's miracles. It is because he is God that he has power to heal the sick (such as the leper, Mark 1:40–41) and raise the dead (such as Lazarus, John 11:1–44), but because he is a man that he feels compassion (Mark 1:41) and weeps (John 11:35).

The human Jesus slept as 'A furious squall came up, and the waves broke over the boat, so that it was nearly swamped', and the experienced fishermen were afraid of drowning. The divine Son of God 'rebuked the wind and said to the waves, "Quiet! Be still!" Then the wind died down and it was completely calm' (Mark 4:35–41).

Paul's sorrow

What is the context of Paul's doxology? The apostle's 'great sorrow and unceasing anguish' in his heart is due to the fact that his own race have rejected their Messiah, the Lord Jesus Christ (Rom. 9:1–3). Paul is distressed because his fellow-Jews neglected their God-given privileges (9:4–5) and because many of his kinsmen did not belong to the true Israel (vv. 6–9).

Only those who trust in Abraham's God for salvation are the true children of Israel. The children of Abraham are those who have the faith of Abraham. This is the reason why 'not all who are descended from Israel are Israel' (v. 6; see also 2:28–29; 4:1–25).

Why do some believe? It is because of God's sovereign grace (vv. 10–21). God said to Moses, 'I will have mercy on whom I have mercy, and I will have compassion on whom I have compassion' (v. 15). Israel rejected God because of their unbelief; however, God used this unbelief to bring salvation to penitent sinners from all nations. Human responsibility and divine sovereignty go hand-in-hand in the Bible.

Moreover, Paul weeps because those who reject Christ are 'cursed' (v. 3). Those—Jews and non-Jews—who will not weep in repentance will weep for ever in hell. Paul wishes that he could enter hell instead of his Jewish family and friends—such is his intensity. He echoes Moses' desire after the incident of the golden calf (Exod. 32:31–33). Yet neither Moses nor Paul could suffer hell on behalf of the lost because both men were sinners themselves. Only the sinless Son of God could die as the substitute of sinners. He took the curse that we deserve: 'Christ redeemed us from the curse of the law by becoming a curse for us' (Gal. 3:13).

The comment of William Hendriksen, twentieth-century American Presbyterian pastor and writer, on Paul's weeping is heart-searching: 'The person who is unconcerned about those who are perishing may well wonder whether he is a Christian.'[3]

How, then, does the doxology of verse 5 relate to its context? The greatest privilege of all was to belong to the nation in which the Messiah was born. The Messiah is the Lord Jesus Christ, who is 'God over all'; therefore, to reject him is to reject God. This rejection, whether by Jews or non-Jews, merits eternal punishment.

Praise

In Romans 1:25 Paul writes about 'the Creator—who is for ever praised'; here, in 9:5, he calls us to praise the divine Saviour. He adds 'Amen' to affirm that what God has planned will happen; nothing can thwart his decrees.

Believers—Jews and non-Jews—will eternally praise God that Christ saved them from the misery of hell and welcomed them into the bliss of heaven.

'I will have mercy'

Every time Thomas Bradwardine (1290–1349) read Romans 9 he paused at verse 15—'I will have mercy on whom I have mercy, and I will have compassion on whom I have compassion'—and remembered how, through that verse, he became a Christian. It was then that he realized that God's grace is a free gift that cannot be earned or bought by our merits or efforts. It was a turning point that changed his preaching. From that time he emphasized that salvation is through Christ alone.

Bradwardine became Chancellor of St Paul's Cathedral, London, in

1337 and in 1349 was appointed Archbishop of Canterbury, a post he held for only thirty-eight days because he died of the Black Death, a bubonic plague that swept through Europe in the fourteenth century.

When Bradwardine visited Oxford, one of his hearers was John Wycliffe, who picked up Bradwardine's emphasis on God's sovereign grace, which he himself then preached at Lutterworth, Leicestershire, from 1374 until his death in 1384. Wycliffe spread this message in two ways: by commissioning itinerate preachers, known as Lollards; and by translating the Bible from the Latin Vulgate version into vernacular English, a task that he completed in 1382. This was the first complete Bible in English.

Notes

1 **William Hendriksen** discusses the various translations of this verse in his *Romans 9–16* (New Testament Commentary; Edinburgh: Banner of Truth, 1981), pp. 315–316.

2 **Charles Hodge,** *Commentary on Romans* (Geneva Commentary; Edinburgh: Banner of Truth, 1989; electronic edn., STEP Files © 2003).

3 **Hendriksen,** *Romans 9–16*, p. 310.

The depth of God's riches (Rom. 11:33–36)

Oh, the depth of the riches of the wisdom and knowledge of God!
How unsearchable his judgments,
and his paths beyond tracing out!
'Who has known the mind of the Lord?
Or who has been his counsellor?'
'Who has ever given to God,
that God should repay him?'
For from him and through him and to him are all things.
To him be the glory for ever! Amen.

T his is one of the greatest doxologies in the Bible, though not often read by preachers after the closing hymn in a service— probably because it runs to sixty-eight words! The apostle Paul bursts into praise even though he is still five chapters away from the end of his letter to the Romans. Before the final 'Amen' at the end of chapter 16, Paul will pen five more ascriptions of praise to God (Rom. 15:5–6, 13, 33; 16:20, 25–27). It was impossible to stop this man praising God!

Paul's amazement

Paul begins this benediction with the word 'Oh', an expression of his breathtaking amazement. Why is the apostle so amazed? Because of God's sovereign grace; this is Paul's theme in chapters 1–11. In these chapters, the apostle explains that we are all sinners deserving God's wrath. However, this holy God's wrath fell on his own sinless Son, the Lord Jesus Christ. He took our sin; he bore God's wrath as he died on the cross. Therefore, God pardons all who come to him through Christ. Who will come? Those who repent of their sins. Who will repent? Those whom God has chosen before the creation of the world. He could have left sinners to reap the consequences of their sin, but, in his mercy, he chose to save some and to send his Son to die for them.

Paul is also amazed because of God's wisdom and knowledge: 'Oh, the depths of the riches of the wisdom and knowledge of God!' God's wisdom is seen in his selection of the best method of achieving his plans. He planned that the only way to save his elect was by the death of his Son as their substitute at Calvary.

God's 'knowledge' is his knowing all things, past, present and future, at a glance. He knows all things because he plans all things. Nothing happens outside his sovereign will. The word 'depth' indicates that the wisdom and knowledge of God are too deep for us to fathom. The rest of verse 33 expands the meaning of 'the depth' of God's wisdom and knowledge.

Believing in God's wisdom and knowledge gives comfort to suffering Christians because they know that he wisely plans all events for their good (Rom. 8:28). His ways may puzzle them, but believers are confident that God knows exactly what he is doing and where he is leading them.

God's judgements

God's judgements are his eternal decrees to save each one of his elect as and when he determines. The phrase 'his paths [are] beyond tracing out' refers to footprints that are untrackable, such as those of an animal that a hunter is unable to follow.

It is the same idea that the psalmist expresses by declaring of God, 'Your path led through the sea, your way through the mighty waters, though your footprints were not seen' (Ps. 77:19). Only God's own Spirit 'searches all things, even the deep things of God' (1 Cor. 2:10).

Who can understand God's plan to save sinners? Unbelievers deride the gospel *message* (salvation through Christ's death on a cross) and its *method* of being communicated (preaching by weak and sinful men). Nevertheless, this is how God has chosen to save his people from their sins!

What is the significance of the word 'riches' in verse 33? God's grace, wisdom and knowledge are an ocean that will never run dry. An old writer quaintly comments, 'As soon as think of emptying the ocean with a cockle shell as think of exhausting the treasures of divine goodness, wisdom and knowledge.'[1] The nineteenth-century commentator Albert Barnes writes,

Riches denote the abundant blessings and mercies which had been conferred on sinful people by the gospel. These were vast and wonderful. The pardon of sin; the atonement; the hope of heaven; the peace of the gospel; all bestowed on the sinful, the poor, the wretched and the dying; all speak of the great mercy and the rich grace of God.[2]

Paul speaks of God's rich grace in his letter to the Ephesians: 'In him we have redemption through his blood, the forgiveness of sins, in accordance with the riches of God's grace that he lavished on us with all wisdom and understanding' (Eph. 1:7–8). He adds, 'God ... is rich in mercy' (Eph. 2:4), and writes about 'the incomparable riches of his grace, expressed in his kindness to us in Christ Jesus' (2:7). God's rich grace can save all sorts of sinners and the worst of sinners (1 Tim. 1:15).

God's mind

In Romans 11:34 Paul poses two questions: 'Who has known the mind of the Lord? Or who has been his counsellor?' He is quoting Isaiah 40:13

from the Septuagint (the Greek translation of the Old Testament). 'The very asking shows that both questions have but one answer: No one! Men can ponder "the mind of the Lord", but only "the Lord" himself can know it.'3 The finite human mind cannot probe the infinite divine mind. Do we have the humility to let God be God? Are we willing to trust him, even when his dealings puzzle us?

The second question in verse 34 reminds us that God has always known everything, so he does not need a teacher. The divine Counsellor gives wisdom and guidance to his people. Remember the psalmist's words: 'The steps of a good man are ordered by the LORD. And He delights in his way. Though he fall, he shall not be utterly cast down; for the LORD upholds him with His hand' (Ps. 37:23–24, NKJV). And again: 'I will instruct you and teach you in the way you should go; I will counsel you and watch over you' (Ps. 32:8). The NKJV translates this last phrase as 'I will guide you with my eye'. We can never stray out of God's sight; he cares for us twenty-four hours a day, every day of our lives, from birth to death.

The third question in verse 35 is a quotation from the Aramaic translation of Job 41:11: 'Who has ever given to God, that God should repay him?' God owes us nothing, yet, in his mercy, he chose us and sent Christ to die for us. Not only do we deserve no favour from him, but actually we are more than worthy of eternal death.

Though we cannot probe God's mind, what we need to know for salvation, sanctification and service God has made known in his Word. To quote Moses, 'The secret things belong to the LORD our God, but the things revealed belong to us and to our children for ever, that we may follow all the words of this law' (Deut. 29:29). We are to follow—obey—his Word.

Adoration

The only response that Paul—and we—can make to God's grace,

wisdom and knowledge is to adore the Lord: 'For from him and through him and to him are all things. To him be the glory for ever! Amen' (Rom. 11:36).

God is the source ('from him'), the sustainer ('through him') and the goal ('to him') of all things. These 'all things' include salvation. We have nothing and are nothing apart from God. Eternal glory belongs to him alone: 'To him be the glory for ever.'

Only those who desire God's glory on earth will sing his praise in heaven. This thrilling doxology ends with an affirmation. 'Amen' means 'so be it' or 'it shall be'.

We may compare Paul in this benediction to a climber who has reached the summit of Mount Everest. He can only stand awestruck at God's beauty and majesty.

Notes

1 **W. Burrows,** *Romans*, vol. xxvi (The Preacher's Homiletical Commentary; Grand Rapids, MI: Baker, 1986), p. 381.
2 **Albert Barnes,** *Notes on the New Testament: Romans* (Grand Rapids, MI: Baker, 1990; electronic edn., STEP Files © 1999, Findex.com).
3 **John MacArthur,** *Romans 9–16*, ch. 10 (MacArthur New Testament Commentary; Chicago: Moody Press, 1995; electronic edn., STEP Files © 1997, Parsons Technology, Hiawatha, IA).

Endurance and encouragement (Rom. 15:5–6)

May the God who gives endurance and encouragement give you a spirit of unity among yourselves as you follow Christ Jesus, so that with one heart and mouth you may glorify the God and Father of our Lord Jesus Christ.

The year is AD 58. It is about twenty-five years since the death of the Lord Jesus Christ. The members of the church in the Imperial City of Rome are wending their way to an extraordinary members' meeting. Once the meeting is under way, one of the believers rises to his feet with an air of solemnity; he obviously has something of great weight on his mind. An expectant hush falls on the assembly.

'I am very distressed that members of this church are eating pork,' the man says.

There is a look of horror on the faces of the Jewish members. Other members from non-Jewish families can hardly restrain their amusement. Soon, members are arguing: some for the perpetual authority of the Mosaic food laws, with others citing Peter's vision at Joppa (Acts 11:4–9).

'God told Peter to eat "unclean food". God's law is greater than Moses' law,' they insist.

'Order!' cries the exasperated chairperson.

Later, the church secretary's head aches as he tries to write the minutes of this disorderly meeting.

'To eat or not to eat' divided believers in first-century Rome. News reached Paul, who responded by telling the Romans, '… the kingdom of God is not a matter of eating and drinking, but of righteousness, peace and joy in the Holy Spirit, because anyone who serves Christ in this way is pleasing to God and approved by men' (Rom. 14:17–18). The word 'righteousness' sums up the apostle's message in Romans: we are not saved by our deeds but by the merits of Christ. Genuine believers desire to live righteous (holy) lives.

We may smile in our smugness at believers coming to blows about pork joints. But what would Paul say about some of the ridiculous arguments that disrupt our churches and dishonour Christ in our church members' meetings?

This disagreement about kosher food forms the background to Paul's three benedictions in Romans 15:5–6, 13, 33. This is why he prayed that 'The God of peace' (v. 33) would give the Romans 'a spirit of unity' (v. 5) and 'all joy and peace' (v. 13). These three benedictions show us how to pray when there is division within a church. If we prayed more and spoke less, we would quickly resolve disputes among believers.

Endurance

Paul asks God to give the Romans 'endurance' (v. 5). Quarrels in a church discourage members and may even stop some from attending worship. We need 'endurance', translated by Hendriksen as 'patient endurance'.[1] We ought to focus on the faithfulness of God, rather than looking too much at the faults of fellow-believers. While we argue, sinners are not hearing the gospel and are therefore in danger of an eternity in hell. It is essential that we continue serving God.

Job is an example of a man of 'patient endurance'. He persistently loved God, even though he suffered physically and sank into a black hole of depression. He still trusted God, despite the bad theology of his 'friends', who told him, 'You are suffering because you are a bad man.' Their assessment contradicted God's view of Job: 'There is no one on earth like him; he is blameless and upright, a man who fears God and shuns evil' (Job 1:8).

Chapter 4

The apostle James links Job's patience with the Lord's overflowing 'compassion and mercy' (James 5:11). A couple of verses earlier he issues the command, 'Don't grumble against each other' (v. 9). Impatient Christians ought to consider the Lord's patience towards them!

How does God give us endurance? As we read and obey his Word. Look at Romans 15:4: 'For everything that was written in the past was written to teach us, so that through endurance and the encouragement of the Scriptures we might have hope.' Paul quotes five Scriptures in this chapter concerning the conversion of the Gentiles (vv. 9–12, 21; they are Ps. 18:49; Deut. 32:43; Ps. 117:1; Isa. 11:10; 52:15).

We read in God's Word, for example in Hebrews 11, of believers who endured. We also read of God's patience with erring saints, such as David and Peter. Reading God's Word stirs up the fire of hope—confidence in God—in our hearts. Paul's words in Romans 15:4 highlight the importance of the Old Testament; these were the only Scriptures available to the Roman Christians before they received Paul's letters.

Encouragement

The Greek word translated as 'encouragement' (Rom. 15:4–5) in the NIV and 'comfort' and 'consolation' in the KJV has links with the word 'Comforter', which is a title of the Holy Spirit. No single word in English is a perfect translation of this word, which means 'to call to one's side'. The God who gives encouragement comes alongside weak and troubled believers when they read the Scriptures. Biblical comfort or encouragement is more than a few soothing platitudes—it is renewed strength to fight against sin and Satan.

The Roman Christians would not have owned personal copies of the Scriptures; how, then, could they receive encouragement from God's Word? They were encouraged as they listened to preaching. Paul, writing to the Thessalonians, says, '... the appeal we make does not spring from error or impure motives' (1 Thes. 2:3); the word 'appeal' is 'exhortation' in the KJV and is the same word translated as 'encouragement' in Romans 15. Preaching should motivate God's people to love and to serve Christ.

'A spirit of unity'

God gives his people endurance and encouragement so that they live in harmony (Rom. 15:5). Jews and Gentiles, the strong and the weak, are to live peacefully in one church. Each group is to accept every member of the other group as Christians: 'Accept one another, then, just as Christ accepted you, in order to bring praise to God' (v. 7).

The phrase 'give you a spirit of unity' in verse 5 reads as 'grant you to be likeminded' in the KJV, but this does not imply uniformity. 'It is not necessary that Christians think exactly alike on every subject. But it is necessary that in the lives of all God's children the love of Christ Jesus be reflected and his will is done.'[2] Christ's will is that we 'Love one another. As I have loved you, so you must love one another. By this all men will know that you are my disciples, if you love one another' (John 13:34–35). God's sinless Son spoke these words after washing the feet of his proud disciples, who had been arguing about which of them was the greatest.

'One heart and mouth'

What is the distinction between 'heart' and 'mouth' in Romans 15:6? 'Heart' points to what we believe and 'mouth' indicates what we say (10:9–10). These terms raise two questions: Do I mean what I say? Do I feel love for fellow-believers in my heart? On the words 'one … mouth', A. W. Pink writes, 'Tongues which are used to backbite one another in private cannot blend together in singing God's praise.'[3] Pink's use of 'backbite' is interesting. The dictionary defines 'backbiting' as 'malicious talk about someone who is not present'.[4] 'Backbiting' suggests a wild dog biting someone. Paul uses the imagery of a ferocious animal in Galatians 5:15: 'If you keep on biting and devouring each other, watch out or you will be destroyed by each other.' To behave in this way implies that we are not Christians at all!

'Follow Christ Jesus'

How can we live peacefully with one another? By following Christ Jesus: we take his life as a role model for our own. We ask questions such as, 'How did Jesus treat those who insulted him and who misunderstood him?'; 'How did he show compassion to the weak and the needy?' To find the answer to these questions, slowly and prayerfully read the four Gospels. Then think about passages such as Philippians 2:1–11 and 1 Peter 2:21–23. To follow Christ is to take 1 Corinthians 13 into the church, the home, the workplace and the community. This is how we bring glory to God (Rom. 15:6). A genuine concern for God's glory ought to settle disputes and controversies among sincere believers.

Finally, look at the last words of Romans 15:6: 'the God and Father of our Lord Jesus Christ'. Why does Paul conclude his benediction with these words? The title 'Jesus Christ' emphasizes the Saviour's human nature. On the other hand, 'Father of our Lord' calls attention to the Son's divine nature. He is God's eternal and uncreated Son. God is our Father, too! We are his children by adoption. Therefore, we should live together in peace as brothers and sisters. God gave Paul endurance and encouragement in his many trials; he is well able to give us these blessings as well.

Notes

1 **William Hendriksen,** *Romans 9–16* (New Testament Commentary; Edinburgh: Banner of Truth, 1981), p. 472.
2 Ibid., p. 473.
3 **Arthur W. Pink,** *Gleanings from Paul: The Prayers of the Apostle* (Chicago: Moody, 1967), p. 33.
4 'Backbiting', at Oxford Dictionaries, www.oxforddictionaries.com; accessed October 2011.

The God of hope (Rom. 15:13)

May the God of hope fill you with all joy and peace as you trust in him, so that you may overflow with hope by the power of the Holy Spirit.

When you receive a cheque you present it to the bank so that you can draw on the money sent to you. A cheque left in your wallet or handbag is of no use. God's promises are like cheques—they are not much use if they are left inside the pages of the Bible. You must take these promises in prayer to the bank of heaven and ask God to give you what he has promised.

Promises, prayer and problems

In Romans 15:9–12, 21 Paul quotes five passages from the Old Testament (Ps. 18:49; Deut. 32:43; Ps. 117:1; Isa. 11:10; 52:15) in which God promises to save Gentiles (non-Jews). God brought Christ into the world within the cradle of the Jewish race, but his mercy is not restricted to that nation. Having reminded the Romans of God's promises, the apostle prays for them to 'the God of hope' (15:13). The prayer to 'the God of hope' in this verse is linked to the promise of hope for all races in verse 12.

The wider context of Paul's benediction is the disagreements among the Romans concerning meat offered to idols; therefore he prays that these believers will know 'joy and peace' in their relationships with one another. The remarks of A. W. Pink are pertinent: 'The closer a company of Christians are drawn to their Lord, the closer they are drawn to one another.'[1]

Chapter 5

The triune God

Though Paul prays to 'the God of hope', his prayer is rooted in his understanding of the three-in-one nature of God. The 'Root of Jesse' (v. 12) is the Messiah: the Lord Jesus, God the Son. The 'God of hope' (v. 13) is clearly God the Father. The apostle prays for the Romans to know 'the power of the Holy Spirit' (v. 13)—God the Holy Spirit, the third Person of the Trinity. Paul does not try to prove the doctrine of the Trinity; nevertheless, his prayers are always within this framework that both the Lord Jesus Christ and the Holy Spirit are equal with God the Father. He places the Son and the Spirit alongside God the Father.

So now we come more directly to Paul's benediction in Romans 15:13.

'The God of hope'

Pink defines biblical hope as 'a firm expectation and confident anticipation of the things God has promised'.[2] How important, then, to have a deeper understanding of who God is and to have a thorough grasp of the Bible so that we know what God has said. Indeed, all that we know about God comes from God himself in his Word.

In his famous *Pilgrim's Progress*, John Bunyan names a character 'Hopeful'. This is a good name for all Christians. By contrast, unbelievers are hopeless because they have no God to whom they can turn and no future to which they can look forward. Paul, in his letter to the saints in Ephesus, describes non-Christians as 'without hope and without God in the world' (Eph. 2:12). On the other hand, writing to Titus, he portrays believers as those who have 'faith and knowledge resting on the hope of eternal life, which God, who does not lie, promised before the beginning of time' (Titus 1:2).

Joy

Joy is emphasized several times in Romans 15; see, for example, verse 9, where we read, 'I will sing hymns to your name'; and verse 10: 'Rejoice, O

Gentiles, with his people.' Paul quotes the psalmist in verse 11: 'Praise the Lord, all you Gentiles, and sing praises to him, all you peoples.' We experience joy because we know God and therefore we are sure that he has forgiven our sins.

We ought to notice that Paul prays for God to 'fill' his readers 'with all joy'. Think of water flowing over the rim of a glass, or a river bursting its banks and flooding the land. This is the joy of which Peter writes: 'Though you have not seen him [Jesus], you love him; and even though you do not see him now, you believe in him and are filled with an inexpressible and glorious joy' (1 Peter 1:8). Was Peter writing about the future? Not at all! This is clear from his words 'though you do not see him now', which are in the context of suffering (vv. 6–7). We praise God even in pain, because an eternal inheritance awaits us (vv. 3–5).

Why do some Christians seem so unhappy? The setting of Paul's benediction suggests one reason: division and disagreements. Another obvious reason is a guilty conscience because of sin. David, after his sin with Bathsheba, prayed, 'Restore to me the joy of your salvation' (Ps. 51:12). Restored joy comes through the sort of heartfelt penitence experienced by David in Psalm 51.

Peace

In Paul's letter to the Romans we read both bad news and good news. The bad news is that we are all sinners who stand guilty before the all-seeing and all-knowing God. We cannot earn God's pardon by our own hard work. God is our enemy; we are rebels against the divine King (3:10–20; 5:10; 8:5–8). The good news is that God sent his Son, Jesus Christ, to reconcile us to himself. God's wrath against sin fell on Christ when he died as our substitute on the cross. God declared him 'guilty' in order to declare us 'not guilty'. We have peace with God through Christ (3:21–26; 5:1–2; 8:31–34).

How shameful that those who have peace with God should be arguing with one another! Christians should pay attention to Paul's teaching about 'brotherly love' in Romans 12:9–21. In verse 18, he writes, 'If it is possible, as far as it depends on you, live at peace with everyone.' The writer to the Hebrews echoes Paul: 'Make every effort to live in peace with all men' (Heb. 12:14). What effort are you making in your neighbourhood and in your church to live at peace with others?

The apostle links joy and peace in Romans 14: 'For the kingdom of God is not a matter of eating and drinking, but of righteousness, peace and joy in the Holy Spirit, because anyone who serves Christ in this way is pleasing to God and approved by men' (v. 17). Believers in Rome debated eating or not eating meat offered to idols and the observance or non-observance of Jewish festivals. Nowadays, believers sometimes disagree over the consumption or non-consumption of alcohol or the use of leisure time. To know 'peace and joy' we must focus on what is essential—salvation in Christ—rather than on issues that are of secondary importance.

Trust

Trust (Rom. 15:13; translated as 'believing' in the KJV) is evidence that we take God's promises seriously. God says that 'Everyone who calls on the name of the Lord will be saved' (Rom. 10:13)—so we go to him asking for the pardon of our sins. The 'everyone' embraces sinners of every culture and race. Christ is 'Lord of all and richly blesses all' (10:12). Having trusted him for salvation, we trust him every day, throughout our lives, for his sustaining grace. We know that he will fulfil the promise of Philippians 1:6: 'he who began a good work in you will carry it on to completion until the day of Christ Jesus.' The 'good work' is his work of grace in saving our souls.

Hope

What is the outcome of God giving us joy, peace and trust? We 'overflow with hope'. The term translated as 'overflowing' is similar to that for 'fill' and depicts a river drenching parched land. Joy, peace and trust flood our souls with hope. We lose joy, peace and trust when we focus too much on our trials and temptations and when discord turns our thoughts away from heaven. However, when we are overflowing with joy, peace and trust, we are confident that God will keep his promises and fulfil his plans. We know that he orders all the circumstances of our lives for our good and his glory (Rom. 8:28).

How does hope differ from trust? Trust believes what God has said; hope expects what God will do.

'The power of the Holy Spirit'

Joy, peace, trust and hope are the fruit of the Holy Spirit. Listing the Spirit's fruit in his letter to the Galatians, Paul includes 'love, joy, peace' (5:22). Writing to the Ephesians, Paul explains that the Holy Spirit's presence within the believer is the pledge of entering the inheritance of heaven (Eph. 1:13–14). Everyone whom God has chosen and for whom Christ died has the seal of the Holy Spirit; all who have the seal will share the inheritance.

Do you want overflowing joy, peace, trust and hope? Then pray that God will fill you with his Holy Spirit (Eph. 5:18). What is the evidence of a Spirit-filled life? It is expressed in praise (5:19–20) and is seen in a Christ-centred marriage (vv. 21–33) and in wise parenting (6:1–4). The Spirit-filled believer is a better employer or employee (6:5–9). It is in these spheres of life that we fight a spiritual warfare (vv. 10–18). The true believer prays for all God's people, but especially for spiritual leaders (vv. 18–20).

'The God of peace'

Paul concludes Romans 15 with a prayer that the believers in Rome will know the presence of the 'God of peace': 'The God of peace be with you all. Amen' (v. 33). God's presence brings endurance, encouragement, harmony, joy, peace and hope. The apostle prays that 'this God of peace may come so close to them that they may experience his peace in their lives, may meditate on it, possess it, rejoice in it'.[3] What better petition could we pray for one another in the churches to which we belong?

Notes

1 **Arthur W. Pink,** *Gleanings from Paul: The Prayers of the Apostle* (Chicago: Moody, 1967), p. 35.

2 Ibid., p. 39.

3 **William Hendriksen,** *Romans 9–16* (New Testament Commentary; Edinburgh: Banner of Truth, 1981), p. 498.

Crushing Satan (Rom. 16:20)

The God of peace will soon crush Satan under your feet. The grace of our Lord Jesus be with you.

T his is surely one of the most encouraging verses in the Bible! This benediction anticipates the defeat of our enemy, the devil. Satan crushed 'under your feet' alludes to conquerors putting their feet on the necks of vanquished rulers.

Like a star, this promise shines brighter when placed against the dark descriptions of Satan in 1 Peter 5:8 and Revelation 12:9–10: 'Your enemy the devil prowls around like a roaring lion looking for someone to devour'; 'The great dragon was hurled down—that ancient serpent called the devil, or Satan, who leads the whole world astray. He was hurled to the earth, and his angels with him … the accuser of our brothers, who accuses them before our God day and night, has been hurled down.' We will crush the lion-dragon under our feet; at last his accusing mouth will be silenced for ever!

Satan—then known as Lucifer—was expelled from heaven to earth, along with other angels who supported him, because of his rebellion against God. On earth he enticed Adam and Eve into disobeying God so that sin, sorrow and death entered the bloodstream of the human race (Isa. 14:12–15; Ezek. 28:11–19; Luke 10:18; Rev. 12:3–4; Rom. 5:12–21). This is the broader context of this benediction-promise.

Teachers of error

What is the immediate context? The saints in Rome (see 1:7) faced the activity of those who claimed to serve 'our Lord Christ' (16:18) but caused divisions and spread erroneous teaching by their lies and their flattery. The naïve were especially vulnerable because the teaching of these evil men seemed so plausible (16:17–18). The naïve ('simple', KJV/NKJV) were the innocent who did not suspect these teachers of deceit. Was Paul thinking of cunning Satan's deception of the innocent Eve (Gen. 3:1–6; 2 Cor. 11:3; 1 Tim. 2:13–14)?

Maybe the mention of these deceivers immediately after the reference to 'a holy kiss' (Rom. 16:16) suggests that they were like Judas, who gave Christ a kiss and then sold him for thirty pieces of silver (Luke 22:47–48; Ps. 41:9). The obedience of the Romans (some of them are named in 16:1–16) stands in contrast to the disobedience of these false teachers (16:19).

Christians, then and now, need spiritual perception to see the obstacles that false teachers throw onto the pathway to heaven (16:17). Therefore, Paul urges his readers to 'be wise about what is good, and innocent about what is evil' (v. 19). These words look back to Jesus's saying: 'I am sending you out like sheep among wolves. Therefore be as shrewd as snakes and as innocent as doves' (Matt. 10:16).

Paul wants the Romans to live in such a manner that they will be equal to the task of choosing what is good in the eyes of God, and that they will be innocent or guileless about doing what is evil. They should be wise for the purpose of doing and promoting what is right, and should not get 'mixed up' with anything that, in God's sight, is wrong.[1]

Paul makes a similar statement in his letter to the Ephesians: 'Be very careful, then, how you live—not as unwise but as wise, making the most of every opportunity, because the days are evil' (Eph. 5:15–16).

The God of peace

To detect false teaching, we also need to remember that 'the final victory is in the hands of the God of peace, not the perpetrators of division. He will shortly tread the devil under our feet. Until then we, as soldiers, are to battle with error. But soon we will receive our discharge, and will stand on the neck of everything satanic [v. 19]'.[2] Meanwhile, we depend on the 'grace of our Lord Jesus' to resist Satan (v. 20).

The title 'God of peace' occurs five times in the New Testament; four of those times are in benedictions (Rom. 15:33; 16:20; Phil. 4:9; 1 Thes. 5:23; Heb. 13:20). The use of this title always relates to the context, as in Romans 16, where the designation 'God of peace' is used to encourage believers coping with discord. The crushing of Satan will bring perfect peace and complete salvation to the saints.

Christ's victory

The affirmation 'God ... will soon crush Satan' refers back to the promise of Genesis 3:15: 'And I will put enmity between you and the woman, and between your offspring and hers; he will crush your head, and you will strike his heel.' Christ is the 'offspring' of the woman (Gal. 3:16) who came to earth through a virgin birth (Gal. 4:4) to defeat Satan and to deliver his elect from the devil's power (Col. 1:13). Genesis 3:15 predicts Christ's defeat of Satan on the cross. To conquer Satan, the conqueror was wounded and crushed.

This promise in Romans 16:20 is true, and therefore reliable, because Christ 'disarmed the powers and authorities, [and] made a public spectacle of them, triumphing over them by the cross' (Col. 2:15). Paul's words picture a conqueror's triumphal procession with the defeated foe being paraded at the rear. The 'powers and authorities' are fallen angels (demons) who rebelled against God their Creator (Col. 1:16). Christ won the decisive victory over the devil, and these fallen angels, at Calvary; he tied up the strong man—Satan—to set his own people free (Mark 3:23–30).

Chapter 6

Sharing Christ's triumph

How will Satan be crushed under the feet of God's people? To some extent, this happens every time we resist temptation—we see him run (James 4:7)! God gives us strength to resist the roaring lion (1 Peter 5:8–9). However, the devil will not be completely crushed until Christ comes again. Christians are co-heirs; they suffer now with Christ and will one day share his glory (Rom. 8:17; 2 Tim. 2:11–13). Already 'we are more than conquerors' (Rom. 8:37); then we will be co-conquerors with him!

The apostle Paul states that God 'will soon crush Satan'. How soon is 'soon'? Over two thousand years have passed and Christ has still not returned. This word 'soon' is like an alarm clock calling us to be spiritually awake so that we are ready for the Saviour's coming: 'The hour has come for you to wake up from your slumber, because our salvation is nearer now than when we first believed' (Rom. 13:11). Besides this, 'soon' reminds us to view the present from the perspective of eternity: conflict with Satan is only for a short time compared with the everlasting joy of the redeemed in heaven. Suffering now prepares us for future glory and is 'not worth comparing with the glory that will be revealed in us' (Rom. 8:18).

Grace

This section of Romans 16 ends with the words 'The grace of our Lord Jesus be with you'. Grace—God's unmerited favour—sums up the message of Paul's letter to the Romans: we are saved by God through faith alone in Christ alone. God declares the penitent not guilty because he declared Christ, his own Son, guilty in their place when he died on the cross. Those who are justified can say, '*our* Lord Jesus'. Each believer knows Christ as a personal Saviour and serves him as Lord. Christ is only the Saviour of those who serve him as Lord.

Paul, in all his thirteen letters, begins with some form of the words 'grace *to you*' (e.g. Rom. 1:7), and ends with 'grace *with you*', as here in this benediction. Why is this? Because Paul, writing God's Word, believed that grace came to his readers through what he wrote. Having heard God's truth, his 'readers will now have to return to the troubles of the world, and he prays that this grace ... will go *with* them'.[3]

Notes

1 **William Hendriksen,** Romans 9–16 (New Testament Commentary; Edinburgh: Banner of Truth, 1981), p. 512.
2 **Stuart Olyott,** The Gospel As It Really Is: Romans Simply Explained (Welwyn Commentary; Welwyn: Evangelical Press, 1979), p. 160.
3 **John Piper,** in **D. A. Carson, (ed.),** Entrusted with the Gospel (Nottingham: Inter-Varsity Press, 2010), p. 19.

Understanding the mystery (Rom. 16:25–27)

Now to him who is able to establish you by my gospel and the proclamation of Jesus Christ, according to the revelation of the mystery hidden for long ages past, but now revealed and made known through the prophetic writings by the command of the eternal God, so that all nations might believe and obey him—to the only wise God be glory for ever through Jesus Christ! Amen.

I don't recall hearing anyone use this benediction at the end of worship. This is probably because it runs to sixty-nine words and is one complex sentence. Now I come to think about it, I cannot remember using this benediction myself! I recollect hearing only one sermon, several years ago, on these verses. No doubt, preachers expounding the book of Romans conclude their series by explaining this benediction. A previous benediction, Romans 11:33–36, is perhaps better known and read more often.

Themes introduced in the first chapter of Romans occur again in this doxology. For example, at 1:11, Paul wants 'to impart [to his readers] some spiritual gift to make [them] strong'; at 16:25, he prays that God will 'establish [them]'. The apostle writes in the first chapter about 'the gospel of God' (1:1) and 'the gospel of his Son' (1:9) which, in the final chapter, he calls 'my gospel' (16:25). The Scriptures also feature in both chapters (1:2; 16:26); so does the emphasis on obedience (1:5; 16:26).

This doxology, 'like a great symphony, leaves a majestic chord sounding in the ears. The music of the Epistle does not weakly fade away.

The final chord is glorious, satisfying and memorable.'[1] What notes do we hear in this ascription of praise?

God's power

Paul planned to travel to Rome on his way to Spain (15:28) but, whether this visit was possible or not, he knew that God, who had saved his people, was 'able to establish' them (16:25). By using the word 'establish', Paul was praying that the Romans would be firmly rooted in the gospel and that God would give them spiritual strength. By God's power they would continue, even if there were no human supports. God strengthens his people through his Word ('the prophetic writings', v. 26) and, especially, as they hear that Word preached ('the proclamation', v. 25).

Notice the link between 'establish' and 'gospel' in verse 25. Those who have a firm grasp of the gospel—the good news of salvation—will remain strong, despite all difficulties. The genuine Christian can say with Paul, 'I know whom I have believed, and am convinced that he is able to guard what I have entrusted to him for that day' (2 Tim. 1:12).

Why did Paul use the phrase 'my gospel'? Because the Lord had revealed and entrusted the gospel to him (Gal. 1:11–17), and because Paul preached it (1 Cor. 15:1–2), shaped his life by it and suffered as a result of it (2 Tim. 2:8–10; 3:8–10).

God's Word

The gospel is 'the revelation of the mystery' (v. 25). The word translated as 'revelation' means 'unveiling'—it is like a curtain pulled back to reveal what previously was unseen. The Greek word translated 'mystery' refers to something hidden in former times but now revealed by God's Spirit.

The apostle writes more fully about this mystery in Ephesians 3:3–6:

… the mystery made known to me by revelation … which was not made known to men in other generations as it has now been revealed by the Spirit to God's holy apostles and prophets. This mystery is that through the gospel the Gentiles are heirs together with Israel, members together of one body, and sharers together in the promise in Christ Jesus.

The mystery was not that the Gentiles (non-Jews) would be saved (this was predicted by the Old Testament prophets, though not fully understood[2]), but that the Gentiles and Jews would be equal heirs in the one body of Christ. The Holy Spirit baptizes both Jews and Gentiles into Christ's body (1 Cor. 12:13). Both Jews and Gentiles worshipped together in Rome.

It is God himself who commanded that this mystery that was 'hidden for long ages past' should now be 'revealed' (16:25–26). The words 'hidden for long ages past' mean 'hidden from eternity in the divine mind'. Paul often presents the idea that the plan of redemption was formed in eternity past (see 1 Cor. 2:6–10; Col. 1:26–27). A similar thought is contained in the word 'command' (16:26), which indicates God's sovereignty in salvation; he 'is in charge of the redemptive work and gives his orders'.[3] The eternal God (v. 26) planned salvation before time, in eternity. We cannot fathom God's ways by human reason, nor can we save ourselves by human effort.

How do we know this 'mystery'? It has been revealed to us 'through the prophetic writings' (v. 26)—God speaks in the Scriptures! The writings of the New Testament apostles are placed alongside those of the Old Testament prophets; this is clear from Peter's words in his second letter (2 Peter 3:15–16). God, who revealed his truth in various ways, progressively through the centuries, has fully and finally spoken in his Son, who is the focus of God's Word from Genesis to Revelation (Heb. 1:1–2; Jude 3; Rev. 22:18–19).

To whom does God speak, and why? To 'all nations', 'so that [they] might believe and obey him' (v. 26). These words look back to Romans 10:11–13: 'As the Scripture says, "Anyone who trusts in [Jesus] will never be put to shame." For there is no difference between Jew and Gentile—the same Lord is Lord of all and richly blesses all who call on him, for, "Everyone who calls on the name of the Lord will be saved"' (see also Isa. 28:16; Joel 2:32). The evidence that we have called on the Lord is that we believe and obey: we trust Christ as our Saviour and serve him as our Lord. The purpose of Christ revealing the mystery was to bring sinners to faith and obedience.

In a previous chapter, Paul, 'the apostle to the Gentiles', wrote about 'the full number of the Gentiles' (Rom. 11:13, 25): a large number from non-Jewish races would be saved. John saw in heaven 'a great multitude that no one could count, from every nation, tribe, people and language, standing before the throne and in front of the Lamb' (Rev. 7:9). So now, Christians are to 'make disciples of all nations' (Matt. 28:18–20), so that believers of all races will understand God's mystery. We go with the authority, and in the power, of God who commanded the mystery to be revealed.

God's messengers

'Jesus Christ' is 'made known through the prophetic writings'. These 'prophetic writings' became part of Paul's gospel through 'the proclamation of Jesus Christ'. The word 'proclamation' depicts the preacher as a herald who declares God's message and who also implores sinners, 'on Christ's behalf', to 'Be reconciled to God' (2 Cor. 5:20).

The method (preaching) and the message (Christ's death for sinners) appear foolish but this is how God has chosen to save sinners and establish saints. Paul had already written to the Corinthians, '... the message of the cross is foolishness to those who are perishing, but to us who are being saved it is the power of God' (1 Cor. 1:18). A few verses later he wrote, 'God was pleased through the foolishness of what was preached to save those who believe ... we preach Christ crucified ... the power of God and the wisdom of God' (vv. 21, 23–24). How did Paul preach Christ?

I did not come with eloquence or superior wisdom as I proclaimed to you the testimony about God. For I resolved to know nothing while I was with you except Jesus Christ and him crucified. I came to you in weakness and fear, and with much trembling. My message and my preaching were not with wise and persuasive words, but with a demonstration of the Spirit's power, so that your faith might not rest on men's wisdom, but on God's power. (1 Cor. 2:1–5)

God's wisdom

Verse 27—'to the only wise God be glory for ever through Jesus Christ! Amen'—brings us back to where this doxology began. It is God's power that is uppermost in Paul's mind in verse 25, whereas in verse 27, the spotlight shines on God's wisdom, especially in the unfolding of his plan to save sinners from all nations.

Hendriksen comments,

The fact that God was able and willing to rescue such sinners fixes Paul's attention on the divine wisdom; that is, on God's ability to employ the best means for the attainment of the highest goal, namely, the glory of God being ascribed to him by the hearts, lives and lips of the redeemed ... It is 'Through Jesus Christ' that the redeemed ascribe never-ending praise to their Benefactor, God Triune ... Paul adds the word of solemn and enthusiastic affirmation and approval, 'Amen.'[4]

Notes

1 **Stuart Olyott,** The Gospel As It Really Is: Romans Simply Explained (Welwyn Commentary; Welwyn: Evangelical Press, 1979), p. 162.
2 See, for example, Rom. 15:8–12.
3 **Archibald Robertson,** Word Pictures in the New Testament, vol. iv, Epistles of Paul (New York: Richard Smith, 1930; electronic edn., STEP Files © 1997, Parsons Technology, Hiawatha, IA).

4   **William Hendriksen,** *Romans 9–16* (New Testament Commentary; Edinburgh: Banner of Truth, 1981), p. 519.

Greetings, grace and love (1 Cor. 16:23–24)

The grace of the Lord Jesus Christ be with you. My love to all of you in Christ Jesus. Amen.

How quickly we sometimes read the closing verses of Paul's letters, such as 1 Corinthians 16:19–24, and miss important spiritual truths! This brief benediction, read in its context, shows us how Paul prayed for believers who, though so gifted (1:5, 7), were quarrelsome (1:10–17; 3:1–23; 11:17–18), immature (3:1–2) and even tainted with the immorality that was rife in the Greek city of Corinth (5:1–13). Nevertheless, the apostle called them 'saints' (1:2, NKJV), thanked God for them (1:4), and prayed in this benediction for God to bless them. Of course, Paul did not ignore their sin; he called them to repentance and to holy living (see, for example, chs. 5 and 6). It is clear from the second letter that his readers took decisive action to discipline an immoral member and to amend their conduct (2:1–11; 7:8–12).

Greetings

Paul, writing in about AD 56, sends greetings to the Corinthians from the 'churches in the province of Asia' (1 Cor. 16:19); these are the seven churches mentioned in Revelation chapters 2 and 3. One of these churches was in Ephesus, where Paul was staying (1 Cor. 16:8). The Ephesian church met in the home of a married couple named Aquila and Priscilla (v. 19), who had lived in Corinth and worked alongside Paul, making tents, when he visited the city (Acts 18:1–3, 18–19). About six years had passed between that visit and his writing his Corinthian letters.

Imagine the joy when the Corinthians received greetings from their former members, Aquila and Priscilla, and especially the apostle Paul, through whose preaching many had become Christians (Acts 18:7–9)! Christian fellowship is a precious jewel.

The curse

Taking the pen from the hand of his amanuensis (1 Cor. 16:21), Paul writes his name to establish the letter's authenticity. Then he adds, 'If anyone does not love the Lord—a curse be on him. Come, O Lord!' (v. 22). These words seem harsh and out of place among the warm and friendly greetings he has just dictated. Picture the quietness—perhaps even shock—within the assembly at Corinth when the members heard Paul's words.

His words—'a curse be on him'—are similar to the imprecations found in several Psalms (e.g. Ps. 109[1]). The KJV reads, 'If any man love not the Lord Jesus Christ, let him be Anathema Maranatha.' 'Anathema', translated in the NKJV as 'accursed', means 'a thing devoted to destruction'. The NIV gives the meaning of the Aramaic word 'Maranatha': 'Come, O Lord!' Both words—Anathema and Maranatha—sound a note of caution.

We ought to notice that Paul is not *predicting* what will happen to those who profess conversion but who in reality do not sincerely love Christ; rather, he is *praying* for God's curse to fall on them because by their conduct they show that they are traitors. The apostle uses similar language in his letter to the Galatians, when writing about 'false brothers [who] had infiltrated our ranks' (Gal. 2:4); of these men he says, '... even if we or an angel from heaven should preach a gospel other than the one we preached to you, let him be eternally condemned! As we have already said, so now I say again: If anybody is preaching to you a gospel other than what you accepted, let him be eternally condemned!' (Gal. 1:8–9). Paul uses such strong language because a false gospel gives sinners a false hope and leads to an everlasting hell.

Roger Ellsworth explains the reason why Paul wrote the words 'a curse be on him' to professing believers:

If the Corinthians continued in their sins, it was evidence that they didn't really love Christ and, therefore, were not truly saved. Are we clear on this? If the general tenor of our lives is disobedience rather than obedience, we don't love Christ, no matter how loudly we may profess to the contrary. And if we don't love Christ, we stand under his condemnation.[2]

It is tragic to be a professing Christian in a church and not to genuinely love the Lord.

Paul is reiterating what Christ himself taught in the Sermon on the Mount:

Not everyone who says to me, 'Lord, Lord,' will enter the kingdom of heaven, but only he who does the will of my Father who is in heaven. Many will say to me on that day, 'Lord, Lord, did we not prophesy in your name, and in your name drive out demons and perform many miracles?' Then I will tell them plainly, 'I never knew you. Away from me, you evildoers!'
(Matt. 7:21–23)

Jesus also taught, in the parable of the sower, that some will profess faith but later their lives will show that they were never really saved (Mark 4:1–20).

'Come, O Lord!'

How will the Corinthians—and professing believers—face the coming Saviour if they have claimed to love him and yet have constantly disobeyed him, or if they have given to him only partial obedience? Verse

22 calls us to examine ourselves. Is our love to Christ genuine? To quote Paul, 'Examine yourselves to see whether you are in the faith; test yourselves' (2 Cor. 13:5; see also 1 Cor. 11:28).

Perhaps in our desire to safeguard the doctrine of God's keeping power we tend to ignore the warnings about a false profession (such as Matt. 7, quoted above) and apostasy (such as Heb. 6). The Puritans emphasized 'the *perseverance* of the saints'. Jesus said, '... he who stands firm to the end will be saved' (Mark 13:13). Those who love Christ will persevere!

'Come, O Lord!' finds an echo in the closing prayer of the Bible, which is a response to Christ's final words to his church: '"Yes, I am coming soon." Amen. Come, Lord Jesus' (Rev. 22:20).

Love for Christ

The first part of 1 Corinthians 16:22—'If anyone does not love the Lord'—prompts a question: Why is it essential to love Christ? Firstly, we ought to love him because he is God and deserves and demands our worship. We should, like Thomas, adore him as 'My Lord and my God!' (John 20:28). Not to love such a glorious Person merits God's everlasting wrath.

Secondly, we ought to love Christ because he is the only Saviour; he alone can save us from God's curse. Jesus himself asserted, 'I am the way and the truth and the life. No one comes to the Father except through me' (John 14:6). Peter declared, 'Salvation is found in no one else, for there is no other name under heaven given to men by which we must be saved' (Acts 4:12). The apostle Paul affirmed, 'For there is one God and one mediator between God and men, the man Christ Jesus' (1 Tim. 2:5).

God's grace

We read in verse 23, 'The grace of the Lord Jesus be with you.' It is because of God's grace—his undeserved mercy—that we love Christ.

Chapter 8

God's grace deepens our love for Christ and strengthens us to persevere as we deal with trials and temptations on the road to the Celestial City. God's grace creates within us a desire to obey God rather than copy the conduct, and accept the morality, of an unbelieving world. Paul prays that the Corinthians will know God's sustaining grace in the wicked city of Corinth.

Paul's love

Despite hurtful criticism from some in Corinth (see 1 Cor. 4), Paul writes with sincerity, 'My love to all of you in Christ Jesus' (1 Cor. 16:24). The apostle displayed in his life what he had written in chapter 13: 'Love is patient, love is kind. It does not envy, it does not boast, it is not proud. It is not rude, it is not self-seeking, it is not easily angered, it keeps no record of wrongs. Love does not delight in evil but rejoices with the truth. It always protects, always trusts, always hopes, always perseveres' (1 Cor. 13:4–7).

It is evident that Aquila and Priscilla shared Paul's love for the Corinthians because he has already mentioned that they 'greet you warmly in the Lord' (16:19). They expressed this love in Ephesus by sharing their home with the church. In the culture of the Middle East, this love for one another was often displayed by 'a holy kiss' (v. 20). In our culture, 'A warm, affectionate handshake or an arm around the shoulder can express the same affection.'[3] Peter exhorted his readers to 'have sincere love for your brothers, love one another deeply, from the heart' (1 Peter 1:22; see also 3:8–9; 4:8). Those who love Christ will love his people!

A few manuscripts omit 'Amen' ('so be it' or 'it will be'); without this, the last word is 'Jesus'. 'The author was acutely conscious that no one is as important as the Saviour. The Lord remains alpha and omega, beginning and end, first and last. In him we have all things; without him there is nothing.'[4]

Notes

1 Psalms 7, 35, 58, 59, 69, 79, 109, 137, 139; see also Neh. 4:4–5; Acts 1:20; 5:1–11; 13:10–11; Gal. 1:8–9; 2 Tim. 4:14–15. A helpful book on this subject is **James E. Adams,** *War Psalms of the Prince of Peace* (Phillipsburg: NJ: P&R, 1991).

2 **Roger Ellsworth,** *Strengthening Christ's Church: The Message of 1 Corinthians* (Welwyn Commentary; Darlington: Evangelical Press, 1995), pp. 269–270.

3 **John MacArthur,** *1 Corinthians* (New Testament Commentary; Chicago: Moody Press, 1984), p. 487.

4 **Peter Naylor,** *1 Corinthians* (EP Study Commentary; Darlington: Evangelical Press, 1996), p. 372.

A Trinitarian benediction (2 Cor. 13:14)

May the grace of the Lord Jesus Christ, and the love of God, and the fellowship of the Holy Spirit be with you all.

There is a wide variety among the biblical benedictions, but one of the best known, used by Christians of all denominations, is Paul's benediction quoted above. But have we taken time to think about the meaning of these words that we hear so often?

Paul's benediction in a nutshell

The seventeenth-century Puritan theologian Thomas Manton (1620–1677) sums up the teaching of this benediction. The apostle is praying 'that God the Father, Son and Holy Spirit will employ all his wisdom, power and goodness to save them from all evil, and bring them to eternal blessedness'. [1]

The Trinity

Paul mentions each Person of the Trinity—Father, Son and Holy Spirit— because each one is active in our salvation. The Father planned salvation, the Son died to save sinners and the Holy Spirit draws them to the Saviour. This concern of each Person of the Trinity makes it certain that no believer will be lost. Christ will save every elect sinner for whom he died.

Paul uses a Trinitarian outline in Ephesians 1: God elected (v. 4), Christ redeemed (v. 7) and the Holy Spirit is the seal given to the believer

(v. 13). The apostle Peter also employs this structure in 1 Peter 1:2. Christians 'have been chosen according to the foreknowledge of God the Father, through the sanctifying work of the Spirit, for obedience to Jesus Christ and sprinkling by his blood'. The word 'foreknowledge' is sometimes misunderstood. It means that God knows everything past, present and future because he has foreordained all events. We are not chosen because God foresaw that we would believe; we believe because he planned that we should believe!

Why does Paul mention the Son, the Lord Jesus Christ, before God the Father? Because this is the order of Christian experience; it is through Christ's grace that we know God's love. Each Person of the Trinity is equally God; to each we must give honour and worship.

So let us now look at each section of this benediction.

The 'grace of the Lord Jesus Christ'

Grace is Christ's pardon of those who deserve eternal punishment because of their sins. Grace was a delightful theme to Paul because of his own conversion on the Damascus road. It never ceased to amaze Paul that he who was once 'a blasphemer and a persecutor and a violent man' was shown God's mercy (1 Tim. 1:13).

Grace is also Christ's power to live the Christian life and to stand firm when going through trials and facing temptations. It is this aspect of grace which is uppermost in Paul's mind in 2 Corinthians 13:14. The Corinthians were under pressure because of false teachers and therefore in great need of sustaining grace (2 Cor. 10–13).

This theme of grace occurs several times in 2 Corinthians. We read, for example, at 8:9, 'For you know the grace of our Lord Jesus Christ, that though he was rich, yet for your sakes he became poor, so that you through his poverty might become rich.' In the next chapter, the apostle reminds his readers that 'God is able to make all grace abound to you, so that in all things at all times, having all that you need, you will abound in every good work' (9:8). These verses are in the context of Christians giving to support fellow-believers in financial need. How could those who had received God's lavish grace be miserly in their giving? And how better to praise God for his 'indescribable gift' (9:15) than through generous giving to God's people?

Furthermore, coping with 'a thorn in the flesh' (a physical disability of some kind), Paul was reassured by God's promise 'My grace is sufficient for you, for my power is made perfect in weakness' (12:9). How did he react when he learnt that, though able to do so, God would not remove this 'thorn'? Having received God's promise, the apostle declared, 'Therefore I will boast all the more gladly about my weaknesses, so that Christ's power may rest on me. That is why, for Christ's sake, I delight in weaknesses, in insults, in hardships, in persecutions, in difficulties. For when I am weak, then I am strong' (vv. 9–10).

In this benediction, Paul gives the Saviour his full title: 'the Lord Jesus Christ'. This title tells us that Jesus is the divine Saviour and Messiah. An angel explained to Joseph that the name Jesus meant 'Saviour' (Matt. 1:20–21). The title 'Christ' means 'anointed'. He fulfilled the Old Testament prophecies that spoke of the Prophet, Priest and King whom God would anoint with his Spirit (Deut. 18:15–22; Ps. 2; 110; Isa. 42:1; 61:1; Luke 4:14–21).

The 'love of God'

Paul prays that the Corinthians will know the comfort of God's love, even when life is hard-going. God displayed his love by giving his Son to die for us while 'we were still sinners' (Rom. 5:8). The apostle wrote about this eternal and unchanging love in Romans 8. In this chapter he dealt with accusations (vv. 33–34) and suffering (vv. 35–37); then he told the Romans that absolutely nothing could defeat them or separate them 'from the love of God that is in Christ Jesus our Lord' (v. 39).

However, a question arises in the mind of the distressed believer: 'If God loves me so much, why does he allow me to suffer?' There are no easy answers, but Hebrews 12:5–11 and 1 Peter 1:3–7 point us in the right direction. These passages, alongside Romans 8, remind us that we are special to God. He loves us more, not less, when we suffer.

Indeed, the writer to the Hebrews, in the passage cited above, views hardship and pain as evidence of God's affection for his children: 'the Lord disciplines those he loves, and he punishes everyone he accepts as a son' (12:6). This discipline is only for 'a little while', and is 'for our good, that we may share in his holiness' (v. 10). Though unpleasant and painful, 'it produces a harvest of righteousness and peace for those who have been trained by it' (v. 11). The ultimate harvest is eternal joy in the presence of Christ in heaven; meanwhile, we joyfully submit to our heavenly Father's discipline (v. 5).

The 'fellowship of the Holy Spirit'

The Holy Spirit convicts unbelievers of sin and then directs them to Christ for salvation (John 16:5–11). The Spirit gives new believers spiritual birth and then takes up residence in their hearts (John 3:5–8; 1 Cor. 6:19–20). Every Christian has the Holy Spirit within from the time of conversion: '… the Spirit of God lives in you. And if anyone does not have the Spirit of Christ, he does not belong to Christ' (Rom. 8:9). The 'Spirit of God' and the 'Spirit of Christ' are both descriptions of God the Holy Spirit, the third Person of the Trinity.

The Holy Spirit assures the believer of God's love, especially in times of trouble. Turning yet again to Paul's letter to the Romans we read, 'God has poured out his love into our hearts by the Holy Spirit, whom he has given us' (Rom. 5:5). Therefore, we may 'rejoice in the hope of the glory of God' and 'also rejoice in our sufferings' (vv. 2–3). Biblical hope is confidence that God will keep his promises.

A few pages later, in Romans 8, in the context of suffering, the apostle states that God's children are 'led by the Spirit of God', who is 'the Spirit of sonship' (vv. 14–15). He gives us the assurance that we are God's children and heirs of God's kingdom. Suffering cannot change our relationship with God. In all our trials, we may run, by prayer, to God our heavenly Father. He will always welcome us! Present pain prepares us for surpassing glory later. In heaven, God will compensate us for our earthly affliction (vv. 16–18).

It is clear from 2 Corinthians 13:14 that Paul wants the Corinthians not simply to have a doctrine of the Holy Spirit but also to know his power and presence every day on their journey to heaven. What is the evidence of his presence and power? It is warm devotion to Christ, godly living and enthusiastic service. Or, to put it another way, it is living the Beatitudes of Matthew 5, displaying the fruit of the Holy Spirit of Galatians 5 and showing the zeal of 1 Corinthians 15:58: '… stand firm. Let nothing move you. Always give yourselves fully to the work of the Lord, because you know that your labour in the Lord is not in vain.'

'Be with you all'

The Father, the Son and the Holy Spirit *will* be with every Christian and with every church. The word 'you' includes those Corinthians who caused Paul so much pain; he holds no grudge against them. Some translations add the word 'Amen', which is 'an expression of faith and an eruption of desire and love'.[2]

To sum up

What more appropriate prayer can be offered at the close of public worship? With hearts uplifted to God it should be pronounced and heard; and every worshipper should leave deeply feeling that what he most needs as he travels on the journey of life; as he engages in its duties, or meets its trials; as he looks at the grave and eternity, is the grace of the Lord Jesus Christ, the love of God, and the blessings which the Holy Spirit imparts.[3]

Notes

1 **Thomas Manton,** *The Complete Works of Thomas Manton*, vol. xix (London: James Nisbet & Co., 1874), p. 156; Manton's *Works* (22 vols.) have been reprinted by Solid Ground Christian Books.

2 Ibid., p. 156.

3 **Albert Barnes,** *Notes on the New Testament: 2 Corinthians* (Grand Rapids, MI: Baker, 1990; electronic edn., STEP Files © 1999, Findex.com).

Praise for the Saviour's death (Gal. 1:3–5; 6:18)

Grace and peace to you from God our Father and the Lord Jesus Christ, who gave himself for our sins to rescue us from the present evil age, according to the will of our God and Father, to whom be glory for ever and ever. Amen.

The grace of our Lord Jesus Christ be with your spirit, brothers. Amen.

A s noted at the start of this book, Paul's benedictions and doxologies are often preceded by what we might call a 'preface'. Galatians 1:5, 'to whom be glory for ever and ever', is a good example of this. The 'preface' that begins in verse 3 is essential to the doxology in verse 5, and provides the reason why we ought to praise 'our God and Father'.

So let us set these verses in their context. Heretical teachers were swarming like bees into the region of Galatia, declaring, 'Unless you are circumcised, according to the custom taught by Moses, you cannot be saved' (Acts 15:1). The message of Paul to the Galatians (written about AD 49) was that salvation is through faith alone in Christ alone, a theme that he developed more fully in his letter to the Romans (written about AD 58). Galatia refers to the southern part of the province, especially the cities of Pisidian Antioch, Iconium, Lystra and Derbe (modern Turkey), visited by Paul during his first missionary journey.

In the opening verses of Galatians, Paul asserts his authority and then defines the true gospel. What is the gospel? It is that God's grace and peace come to us 'from God our Father and the Lord Jesus Christ' because of Christ's death (1:3–4). Only this message brings eternal glory to God the Father (v. 5).

Grace and peace

Grace is God's gift to the bad; it is not his reward for the good. No one is ever good enough for God; we can never earn or buy God's favour. Nevertheless, God himself forgives our sin—this is grace! We are spiritually dead; God gives us eternal life. We are condemned sinners; God justifies us—he declares us not guilty. What do we deserve? Hell. What will God give us? Heaven!

Peace is reconciliation with God. We are 'sinners in the hands of an angry God', to quote the title of a sermon preached by the eighteenth-century American pastor and theologian Jonathan Edwards.[1] God is angry with us because of our sins (Ps. 7:11; Rom. 1:18; Eph. 2:3). He grants us pardon because his wrath fell on his own Son at Calvary.

The Saviour's death

In Galatians 1:3–4 the apostle Paul gives us four facts about the Saviour's death.

1. CHRIST DIED BECAUSE OF THE ETERNAL PLAN OF GOD

'Christ … gave himself … according to the will of our God and Father.' God the Father planned the death of his Son before the creation of the world, and, therefore, before the sin of Adam. Several Scriptures support this statement of Paul's, including Acts 2:23: 'This man was handed over to you by God's set purpose and foreknowledge; and you, with the help of wicked men, put him to death by nailing him to the cross.' 'Foreknowledge' means more than simply what God foresees; it is what he foreordains. He foresees what he has planned. God's unalterable decrees do not cancel out human responsibility. Peter called the murderers of Jesus 'wicked' for crucifying Christ. Later, Peter and the other Christians praised God that 'Herod and Pontius Pilate' and 'the people of Israel … did what [God's] power and will had decided beforehand should happen' (Acts 4:27–28; see also Eph. 1:11; 1 Peter 1:20; Rev. 13:8).

God not only planned the death of his Son, he also chose those for whom Christ died:

He [God] chose us in him [Christ] before the creation of the world to be holy and blameless in his sight. In love he predestined us to be adopted as his sons through Jesus Christ, in accordance with his pleasure and will—to the praise of his glorious grace, which he has freely given us in the One he loves. (Eph. 1:4–6)

Charles Hodge commented, 'If men are chosen to be holy, they cannot be chosen because they are holy … It follows that holiness is the only evidence of election. For one who lives in sin to claim to be elected unto holiness is a contradiction.'[2]

We read in Romans 8:31–32, 'God … did not spare his own Son, but gave him up for us all.' Who are the 'all'? Those whom God 'predestined … called … justified' and who will be 'glorified' (v. 30)—it is for them alone that Christ died.

2. CHRIST DIED WILLINGLY

'Christ … gave himself.' Christ willingly agreed with, and carried out, the Father's sovereign decree, fully knowing the humiliation and pain that would result from this choice. Jesus said, 'The reason my Father loves me is that I lay down my life—only to take it up again. No one takes it from me, but I lay it down of my own accord. I have authority to lay it down and authority to take it up again. This command I received from my Father' (John 10:17–18). There is perfect harmony between the will of the Father and the will of the Son.

The apostle Paul emphasized the willing obedience of Christ in his letter to the Philippians:

... Christ Jesus:

Who, being in very nature God,

did not consider equality with God something to be grasped,

but made himself nothing,

taking the very nature of a servant,

being made in human likeness.

And being found in appearance as a man,

he humbled himself

and became obedient to death—even death on a cross!   (Phil. 2:5–8)

To die 'on a cross' meant 'becoming a curse for us', as Paul wrote in Galatians 3:13, quoting Deuteronomy 21:22–23. Hendriksen comments,

In its Old Testament context, however, this passage does not refer to death by crucifixion, which was not known among the Israelites as a mode of capital punishment. It refers, instead, to the custom according to which, after a wrong-doer had been executed, his dead body was nailed to a post or tree. But if, in the sight of God, the hanging of a *dead* body was a curse, how much more would not the slow, painful and shameful death by crucifixion of a living person be a curse, especially when the dying one was experiencing anguish beyond the power of description![3]

Why did Christ willingly become a curse? Because of his love for his Father and because of his love for his elect. Paul adored 'the Son of God, who loved me and gave himself for me' (Gal. 2:20).

3. CHRIST DIED AS OUR SUBSTITUTE

'Christ ... gave himself for our sins.' 'For the wages of sin is death' (Rom. 6:23); but Christ was not a sinner, so why did he receive sin's wages? He took the wage packet instead of penitent sinners. He died the death that we deserve. He died as our substitute.

The substitutionary atonement of Christ was the doctrine of the prophets and apostles. For example, some seven hundred years before Calvary, Isaiah wrote about Christ,

> But he was pierced for our transgressions,
>> he was crushed for our iniquities;
> the punishment that brought us peace was upon him,
>> and by his wounds we are healed.
> We all, like sheep, have gone astray,
>> each of us has turned to his own way;
> and the LORD has laid on him
>> the iniquity of us all.
>
> (Isa. 53:5)

The apostles Paul, Peter and John taught the same doctrine: 'God made him who had no sin to be sin for us' (2 Cor. 5:21). Christ took not the stain of sin but the sentence of sin. God treated his own Son as the sinner so that he might treat us as righteous. Peter declares, 'He himself bore our sins in his body on the tree' (1 Peter 2:24; see also 3:18). John picks up this theme too: 'He himself is the propitiation for our sins' (1 John 2:2, NKJV). Propitiation means placating God's wrath; Christ did this by taking our sin and bearing God's wrath, as our substitute, when he died on the cross.[4]

These statements reflect Jesus's own understanding of his death: 'For even the Son of Man did not come to be served, but to serve, and to give his life as a ransom for many' (Mark 10:45; compare Matt. 26:28; Luke 22:19–20). The word 'ransom' means an 'exchange'. 'A ransom was originally the price paid for the release of a slave. Jesus, then, is saying that he came into this world to give his life—that is, himself ... in exchange for many.'[5]

4. CHRIST DIED 'TO RESCUE US FROM THE PRESENT EVIL AGE'

The word translated 'rescue' is used in the Acts of the Apostles to describe the setting-free of the Israelites from Egyptian slavery (7:34), the angel delivering Peter from prison (12:11) and the rescue of Paul from an infuriated mob (23:27). Christ has set us free from bondage to sin and to the law—this is the keynote of Paul's letter to the Galatians (see, for instance, 5:1).

John Stott explains the meaning of 'the present evil age':

The Bible divides history into two ages, 'this age' and 'the age to come' ... 'The age to come' has come already, because Christ inaugurated it, although the present age has not yet finally passed away. So the two ages are running their course in parallel. They overlap one another. Christian conversion means being rescued from the old age and being transferred into the new age, 'the age to come' ... The purpose of Christ's death, therefore, was not only to bring forgiveness, but that having been forgiven, we should live a new life, the life of 'The age to come'. And the Christian life is living in this age the life of the age to come.[6]

Those who belong to 'the age to come' set their 'minds on things above, not on earthly things'. It is because they are heavenly minded that they 'Put to death ... whatever belongs to [their] earthly nature' (Col. 3:1–5). Godliness is the hallmark of those who have been rescued from 'the present evil age'.

Praise

Reflecting on Christ's death moves Paul to praise God: 'to whom be glory for ever and ever. Amen' (Gal. 1:5). The authentic gospel, and the genuine Christian, exalts Christ alone. We have nothing in ourselves about which to boast.

Final words

Paul, who began this letter by writing about grace (1:3), returns to this theme in the closing verse: 'The grace of our Lord Jesus Christ be with your spirit, brothers. Amen' (Gal. 6:18). Paul uses 'your'—plural in the original Greek—to emphasize the unity that exists among God's people, with their different ethnic and social backgrounds. At the foot of the cross, 'There is neither Jew nor Greek, slave nor free, male nor female, for you are all one in Christ Jesus' (3:28). There is only one Saviour and only one gospel.

Notes

1 **Jonathan Edwards,** *God at Work?*; a simplified and abridged version of 'The Distinguishing Marks of a Work of the Spirit of God' and the sermon 'Sinners in the Hands of an Angry God' (London: Grace Publications, 1995), pp. 77–91.

2 **Charles Hodge,** *Commentary on the Epistle to the Ephesians* (Geneva Commentary; Edinburgh: Banner of Truth; electronic edn., STEP Files © 2003, QuickVerse).

3 **William Hendriksen,** *The Epistle to the Galatians* (London: Banner of Truth, 1968), pp. 130–131.

4 See **John Murray,** *Redemption, Accomplished and Applied* (London: Banner of Truth, 1961), pp. 29–33.

5 **William Hendriksen,** *The Gospel of Mark* (Edinburgh: Banner of Truth, 1975), p. 415.

6 **John Stott,** *The Message of Galatians* (Bible Speaks Today; Leicester: Inter-Varsity Press, 1968), p. 18.

Beyond our imagination (Eph. 3:20–21)

Now to him who is able to do immeasurably more than all we ask or imagine, according to his power that is at work within us, to him be glory in the church and in Christ Jesus throughout all generations, for ever and ever! Amen.

In the same year that George VI died and Elizabeth II became Queen—1952—a clergyman named J. B. Phillips wrote a book called *Your God Is Too Small*. Phillips, a writer and broadcaster who died in 1982, was best known for his *New Testament in Modern English*, published in 1958 and extremely popular for some years afterwards. We may not agree with some of Phillips' theology; nevertheless, his book title reminds us that sometimes we behave as if God is too small or too weak to help us in our troubles. For example, if I am struggling with discouragement and depression, how does my knowledge of God help me to cope? Depression springs to mind because J. B. Phillips struggled with depression for the last twenty years of his life.

Paul's prayer for the Ephesians (3:14–19) prompts his praise to God (3:20–21). Paul reaches the limits of human language at the end of verse 19 when he prays, 'that you may be filled to the measure of all the fullness of God'. What else can Paul do but adore God?

The triune God

Paul's prayer and benediction have a Trinitarian context. The 'him' of verse 20 is 'the Father' of verse 14. 'Christ Jesus' (v. 21) is the Son who lives in our hearts (v. 17), and whose love 'surpasses knowledge' (v. 19).

God's power works within us (v. 20) through the Holy Spirit (v. 16). Each person of the Trinity works for us and in us as we face the pressures of an ungodly world.

God's power

God 'is able' (v. 20)—he is powerful enough to give us whatever we ask. Does Paul use this expression because of our lack of faith? For example, do we pray for the conversion of a relative or a friend but doubt if it is really possible for that person to be saved? We forget that God saved the self-righteous Paul, the murderer of Christians, so that he later thought of himself as the worst of sinners (1 Tim. 1:15) and 'the least of all God's people' (Eph. 3:8).

What is God able to do?

- What we ask
- All that we ask
- Beyond what we ask
- More than we can even imagine

The words 'immeasurably more than all we ask or imagine' (v. 20) remind me of music that begins softly and calmly, such as Ravel's *Boléro*, perhaps with just one solo instrument playing; then, as the music continues, other musicians begin to play and the volume increases, until there is a crescendo of exciting music filling the concert hall. Paul's words cover every possible need and all circumstances! We grasp that God can give us 'all we ask', and slowly we realize that he answers prayers that we have hardly dared to imagine!

What is the difference between 'ask' and 'imagine'? 'Ask' is what we consider possible, but 'imagine' means what is impossible according to our human reasoning. God can do the impossible, as he did for Mary, the mother of our Lord Jesus Christ. When the angel Gabriel announced to her that she would give birth to the Son of God, she replied, 'How will this be, since I am a virgin?' The angel replied that 'nothing is impossible with God' (Luke 1:30–37). Mary was thinking in terms of human power. God worked in Mary so that she expected God to do the impossible and bring his Son into the world through a virgin birth.

As we pray, God works in us by his Holy Spirit—this is the meaning of Paul's words 'according to his power that is at work within us'. This power working in us raised Christ from physical death and brings believers to life from spiritual death. God will one day raise us from our graves and welcome us into heaven (Eph. 1:19–20; 2:1, 5; 1 Cor. 15:51–57).

A man who knew God's power was John Calvin, the sixteenth-century French Protestant Reformer. Preaching on the closing verses of Ephesians 3, he said that unbelievers

grant readily enough that God is almighty, yet at the same time they do not trust to him in the slightest. It seems to them that he takes his rest in heaven, or else that he does not order things in this world … But, on the contrary, when God speaks to us of his power, it is … that we should make it our shield against all the distresses, [and] hindrances … which the devil casts before our eyes to make us distrust God's promises to us.[1]

God's glory

Why does God answer our prayers? Why does he give us his power? To enhance his glory through us! Look at Paul's statement in verse 21: 'to him be glory in the church'. The apostle desires that the Ephesians will receive and experience all that he has prayed for them. But there is something he wants much more than that. He wants God to be glorified. He wants all creatures everywhere to think high thoughts about God.

Where does God enhance his glory? In you and me—'the church'! Who belongs to God's church? Those who are chosen by God, redeemed by Christ and indwelt by the Holy Spirit (Eph. 1:3–4, 7, 13–14). In this letter to the Ephesians, Paul depicts the church as a state (2:19), a family (2:19; 3:15), a temple (2:20–22), a body (4:4) and an army (6:10–20). Applying these metaphors in local churches glorifies God.

Chapter 11

We glorify God 'in Christ Jesus'; biblical religion is Christ-centred. We honour him as we proclaim, clearly and boldly, salvation through Christ alone and as we display his grace in our lives. We will glorify him 'throughout all generations, for ever and ever'. The final word of this benediction, 'Amen', means 'so be it'—even though the glories of heaven are beyond what we can imagine!

Note

1 **John Calvin,** *Sermons on Ephesians* (Edinburgh: Banner of Truth, 1973), p. 306. Calvin preached these sermons in Geneva from 1558 to 1559, when he was forty-nine years old. They were printed in French in 1562 and then in English in 1577. To find out more about Calvin, read **Kenneth Brownell,** *Travel with John Calvin: Geneva's Minister Whose Thinking Changed the World* (Leominster: Day One, 2009).

Four essential words (Eph. 6:23–24)

Peace to the brothers, and love with faith from God the Father and the Lord Jesus Christ. Grace to all who love our Lord Jesus Christ with an undying love.

'Peace', 'love', 'faith' and 'grace' are four essential words from the benediction with which Paul concludes his letter to the Ephesians. Why are these four words essential? Because they:

- Sum up the message of Paul's letter to the Ephesians.
- Crystallize the gospel.
- Tell us how to live as Christians.
- Express Paul's concern for the Ephesians. Though suffering as a prisoner and unsure if he would leave his cell alive (see Phil. 1:19–24), the apostle prayed for the believers in Ephesus. He was more concerned about their spiritual needs than about his own physical well-being.

Understanding the doctrine contained in these four words made Paul the prisoner richer than the Roman emperor. We too are rich if we have peace, love, faith and grace!

The source

Paul states plainly where peace, love, faith and grace come from: 'God the Father and the Lord Jesus Christ' (v. 23). These are the gifts of God the Father to his adopted children, who are 'dearly loved' (5:1). God is good to all (Matt. 5:45), but he delights to bestow special favours on his own children (Rom. 8:32). His gifts come to us because of the perfect life and atoning death of 'our Lord Jesus Christ' (Eph. 6:24). He is 'ours' through sovereign grace and saving faith (2:4–9).

We see yet again in this benediction that Paul asserts the equality of the Father and the Son. 'The Father and the Son are united as objects of worship and the source of spiritual and saving blessing.'[1] We should also notice the references to God the Holy Spirit in Ephesians (1:13–14, 17; 2:18, 22; 3:5, 16; 4:3–4, 30; 5:18; 6:17–18).

The meaning

We may compare these four essential words to four movements in a symphony. Just as recurring themes are heard throughout a symphony, so these four words recur in the six chapters of Ephesians, and some are found together in verses such as 1:15 and 3:17, where the apostle mentions faith and love. Let us listen to the music of each word so as to understand its meaning.

PEACE

This word occurs eight times in Paul's letter to the Ephesians (1:2; 2:14–15, 17; 4:3; 6:15, 23). Peace is a Person, 'Christ Jesus', through whom old racial barriers are broken down (2:13–15, 17). Peace unites believers from different cultures and diverse lifestyles into the one body of Christ (4:3–6). The members of this 'one body' are soldiers who proclaim 'the gospel of peace' to those who are rebels against God (6:15). We are also in the family of God; therefore, we are 'brothers' and should live in peace with one another (6:23). When the herdsmen of Abraham and the herdsmen of his nephew Lot argued, Abraham said to Lot, 'Let's not have any quarrelling between you and me ... for we are *brothers*' (Gen. 13:8, emphasis added). It is a disgrace when spiritual brothers and sisters squabble with one another.

LOVE

The word 'love' occurs twenty-three times in this letter (1:4, 6, 15; 2:4; 3:17–19; 4:2, 15–16; 5:1–2, 25, 28, 33; 6:23–24). It was because of unmerited love that God chose believers before time (1:4), and because of love that Christ died for them on the cross (2:4). Divine love is beyond human understanding. We know something of Christ's love, and yet we do not fully know it (3:17–18)! Genuine love reveals itself by compassion and patience towards fellow-believers (1:15; 4:15–16). Loving others is not easy, hence Paul's exhortation 'Make every effort to keep the unity of the Spirit through the bond of peace' (4: 3). Christ's love is the model for Christians in the church and for husbands and wives in the home (5:1–2, 25, 28, 33). The best kind of obedience and children's honouring of their parents springs from love; this is implied rather than explicitly stated at 6:1–2.

FAITH

'Faith' is used eight times by the apostle (1:15; 2:8; 3:12, 17; 4:5, 13; 6:16, 23). Faith is taking God at his Word; we believe that he will save us and that he will keep us until we reach heaven. Hebrews 11 tells the stories of godly men and women who lived by faith.

In Ephesians, faith is seen as the door into the Christian life (1:15; 2:8). Faith in Christ gives us confident access to God (3:12). Faith is a vital ingredient for spiritual growth (3:17; 4:13) and a crucial weapon in spiritual warfare (6:16). Those who have true faith will remain faithful to Christ, like Tychicus, the 'faithful servant' (6:21), whom Paul sent to 'the faithful' Ephesians (1:1).

What is the significance of 'one faith' in 4:5? It is what we believe rather than saving faith in Christ. Christians are united in the basic doctrines of the gospel. 'They all receive the Scriptures as the Word of God, and acknowledge themselves subject to their teachings. They all recognize and worship the Lord Jesus as the Son of God. They all trust to his blood for redemption and to his Spirit for sanctification.'[2] This interpretation finds support in Jude's explanation for writing his short letter: 'Dear friends, although I was very eager to write to you about the salvation we share, I felt I had to write and urge you to contend for the faith that was once for all entrusted to the saints' (Jude 3). The 'one faith' is 'the apostles' teaching' to which the early church 'devoted themselves' (Acts 2:42); it is 'the sound doctrine' that Paul entrusted to his assistants Timothy and Titus (1 Tim. 1:10; 2 Tim. 1:13–14; Titus 1:9; 2:1).

GRACE

'Grace'—God's undeserved favour—appears eleven times in Ephesians (1:2, 6–7; 2:5, 7–8; 3:2, 7–8; 4:7; 6:24). Paul writes about God's 'glorious grace' and 'the riches of God's grace that he lavished on us' (1:6, 7–8). Grace saves sinners (2:5, 7–8) and humbles saints (3:8). God uses Christians who regard themselves as 'less than the least of all God's people' (3:8). This may sound like bad grammar, but it is excellent theology! It is grace that equips us for service: 'But to each one of us grace has been given as Christ apportioned it' (4:7). Christ equips all the members of his body to fulfil whatever tasks he has appointed for them.

It is evident that the Ephesians had already experienced peace, love, faith and grace. Paul prays in this benediction that they will know these blessings at a deeper level in their lives and in the church.

The result

Those who know peace, love, faith and grace 'love our Lord Jesus Christ with an undying love' (6:24). Bible translators have rendered the phrase 'with an undying love' in various ways: 'love … in sincerity' (KJV/NKJV); 'with undying and incorruptible [love]' (Amplified Bible); and 'with love incorruptible' (ESV). A. T. Robertson defines the word as 'a never diminishing love'.[3] Hodge defines this love as 'adoring admiration of his person, desire for his presence, zeal for his glory, and devotion to his service'.[4] It is a love for Christ that is permanent and genuine.

John Knox, the sixteenth-century Scots Reformer, loved Christ with a sincere and undying love. As he lay dying, he focused his thoughts on his precious Saviour by reading John Calvin's forty-eight sermons on Ephesians.[5] What a delightful way to enter the presence of the Lord Jesus Christ!

Notes

1 **Charles Hodge,** *Commentary on the Epistle to the Ephesians* (Geneva Commentary; Edinburgh: Banner of Truth, 1991; electronic edn., STEP Files © 2003, QuickVerse).

2 Ibid.

3 **Archibald Robertson,** *Word Pictures in the New Testament,* vol. iv, *Epistles of Paul* (New York: Richard Smith, 1930; electronic edn., STEP Files © 1997, Parsons Technology, Hiawatha, IA).

4 **Hodge,** *Ephesians.*

5 According to the flyleaf of **John Calvin,** *Sermons on Ephesians* (Edinburgh: Banner of Truth, 1973).

Riches in Christ (Phil. 4:19–20, 23)

And my God will meet all your needs according to his glorious riches in Christ Jesus. To our God and Father be glory for ever and ever. Amen … The grace of the Lord Jesus Christ be with your spirit. Amen.

Writing from a prison in Rome, sometime between AD 61 and 64, and facing the possibility of execution, the apostle Paul urged the Philippians to rejoice. The words 'joy' and 'rejoice' appear fourteen times in this brief letter and references to Christ (including pronouns) are found sixty times in its 104 verses. It is obvious that Christ, not circumstances, was the foundation of Paul's joy.

How could Paul experience contentment and joy in a dark and damp prison? Because he knew that God would supply all his needs 'according to his glorious riches in Christ Jesus'. In Philippians 4:19 the apostle links 'my God' with 'all your needs'; the almighty Creator of the world and the sovereign of the universe cares about you and your problems.

I think that the affirmation of verse 19 is an essential part of the benedictions of verses 20 and 23, and it is an appropriate way to conclude corporate worship. Verse 19 is not only a suitable benediction but also a promise that directs our thoughts towards the generous God.

A personal God

Paul was confident that no need would prove beyond the capacity of the God he knew well enough to call 'my God'. Paul's relationship with God was similar to that of David, who wrote, 'The LORD is *my* shepherd, I shall not be in want' (Ps. 23:1, emphasis added). Do you know God in this personal way? If not, this promise does not belong to you. You are instead like a person trying to cash a cheque made payable to someone else! If, however, you are a Christian, are you living in the enjoyment of this wonderful promise?

An emphatic promise

Paul confidently asserts that 'my God *will* meet all your needs' (emphasis added). Reminiscing, David wrote, 'I was young and now I am old, yet I have never seen the righteous forsaken or their children begging bread' (Ps. 37:25). Earlier in that psalm he wrote, 'Better the little that the righteous have than the wealth of many wicked' (v. 16). David, like Paul, had 'learned the secret of being content in any and every situation' (Phil. 4:12).

Discontent comes from wanting more than our 'needs'. God has promised to give us each day 'our daily bread', just as he gave the manna each day to the wandering Hebrews in the wilderness (Matt. 6:11; Exod. 16). God is so benevolent that he often gives more than we need. The words of the psalmist spring once again to mind: 'Blessed be the Lord, who daily loads us with benefits, the God of our salvation!' (Ps. 68:19, NKJV). A wise man prayed,

> ... give me neither poverty nor riches,
> but give me only my daily bread.
> Otherwise, I may have too much and disown you
> and say, 'Who is the LORD?'
> Or I may become poor and steal,
> and so dishonour the name of my God.   (Prov. 30:8–9)

The contented person will enjoy God's peace (Phil. 4:6–7, 9).

A comprehensive promise

Let's think now about the word 'all' in Philippians 4:19: 'God will meet *all* your needs.' The Amplified Bible reads, 'your *every* need' (emphasis added). Whatever the need, God can meet it. He is not like the hole-in-the-wall cash dispenser that occasionally runs out of money or malfunctions. God's supply of grace never runs out. Nor does his ability to answer our prayers! We may weary God with our sins, but we can never tire him with our requests. Sometimes we tire of asking and therefore don't receive; or perhaps we ask selfishly, as James reminds us: 'You do not have, because you do not ask God. When you ask, you do not receive, because you ask with wrong motives, that you may spend what you get on your pleasures' (James 4:2–3).

An inexhaustible promise

The word 'meet' is an interesting one that is translated as 'supply' in the NKJV. The Greek means 'to fill to overflowing' and is translated as 'supplied' in verse 18 in the NIV: 'I am amply supplied, now that I have received from Epaphroditus the gifts you sent.' God would give to the Philippians more than they had given to the apostle Paul. Warren Wiersbe paraphrases Paul: 'You met my need, and God is going to meet your need. You met *one* need … My God will meet *all* your needs. You gave out of your *poverty*, but God will supply your needs out of his *riches* in glory.'[1] God often supplies the needs of his people through fellow-Christians.

'Meet' means that God gives generously, so you cannot ask for too much or too often. To quote James, 'God … gives generously to all without finding fault' (James 1:5). He will not chide you when you keep asking! Jesus made the same point in the parable of the friend at midnight. The man asks for 'three loaves' but receives 'as much as he needs'. Yet the friend woken up at midnight is reluctant to give; by contrast, God delights to give! Jesus adds a promise to the parable: 'Ask and it will be given to you; seek and you will find; knock and the door will be opened to you' (Luke 11:5–10).

How does God give? 'According to his glorious riches in Christ Jesus' (Phil. 4:19). God supplies our needs 'not merely *out of* his riches (as a millionaire might do when he donates a trifling sum to a good cause, subtracting the amount from his vast possessions) but *according to* his riches, so that the gift is actually in *proportion* to God's infinite resources!'[2] God's bounty comes 'in Christ Jesus'; that is, because of his merits. We can never exhaust God's ability or God's willingness to bestow whatever we ask of him.

Commentators debate the meaning of 'glorious' (v. 19); this is reflected in the various translations. Paul is not writing in that verse about God's glory or the glory of heaven, but rather how the Lord deals with the needs of his people on earth. His giving is glorious, meaning that his gifts are lavish and inexhaustible; he is a generous God.

Benedictions

Whenever doctrine fills Paul's mind (as it does in v. 19), it moves his heart to praise (as in vv. 20, 23). Doctrine and praise also prompt love for God's people, expressed in his greetings from 'All the saints' in Rome to 'all the saints' in Philippi (vv. 22, 21).

In verse 19, Paul writes about 'my God', but in verse 20 he adores 'our God'—God is the Father of all believers. The apostle earnestly yearns that God's people will give never-ending praise to their God. The two 'Amen's (vv. 20, 23) are 'the spontaneous utterance of the heart redeemed by grace'.[3]

Grace comes through 'the Lord Jesus Christ' alone (v. 23). He is God ('Lord') who became man ('Jesus') and was anointed (the meaning of 'Christ') by the Holy Spirit. We will worship God our Father and Jesus our Saviour 'for ever and ever' (v. 20).

The phrase 'with your spirit' (v. 23) looks back to 1:27 and 2:2, and highlights the apostle's concern that the whole church be united in Christ. He had pleaded with Euodia and Syntyche, and other quarrelling members, to 'agree with each other in the Lord' (4:2). We ought to focus on the gracious God who supplies all our needs, rather than find fault with one another.

Notes

1 **Warren Wiersbe,** *Be Joyful* (Amersham-on-the-Hill: Scripture Press, 1987), p. 146.
2 **William Hendriksen,** *Philippians* (New Testament Commentary; London: Banner of Truth, 1962), pp. 209–210.
3 Ibid., p. 210.

Harmony and holiness (1 Thes. 3:11–13)

Now may our God and Father himself and our Lord Jesus clear the way for us to come to you. May the Lord make your love increase and overflow for each other and for everyone else, just as ours does for you. May he strengthen your hearts so that you will be blameless and holy in the presence of our God and Father when our Lord Jesus comes with all his holy ones.

The apostle Paul, though a single man, compared himself to 'a mother caring for her little children' and to a tender, wise father (2:7, 11) because many of the Thessalonians had entered God's family through his preaching. Paul visited the city of Thessalonica, capital of the Roman province of Macedonia, on his second missionary journey (Acts 17:1). His visit sparked off a riot! The 'rent-a-mob' gang hired by the Jewish leaders chased Paul and his companion, Silas, out of Thessalonica within three weeks. With tears in his eyes Paul left his spiritual children to fend for themselves.

Paul wrote of being 'torn away' (2:17); he felt like a mother bereaved of her children, such was his intense emotion when he thought of the Thessalonians. Since his hurried departure (about a year before this first letter was written), Paul had prayed constantly for his spiritual children (1:2; 3:10). He also sent Timothy, his trusted assistant, to obtain news about the infant church (3:1–5). How impatiently Paul waited for his return! How eagerly he opened the door when Timothy came back! Imagine Paul's delight when Timothy spoke about the faith, love and endurance of the Thessalonians (1:3)! Timothy's glowing report stimulated Paul's praise and prayer (3:9–13). The outcome of this good news was that Paul wrote from Corinth to encourage the believers and to clear up confusion concerning Christ's second coming; every chapter highlights this theme.

Paul's two benedictions in this first letter (3:11–13; 5:23–24, 28) express his heartfelt desire for the Thessalonians and provide the preacher with appropriate petitions with which to conclude worship and an example of how spiritual leaders should pray for God's people.

God's timing

Paul does not ask God for respite from persecution (3:7); rather he commends his dear children to the care of 'our God and Father himself and our Lord Jesus' (v. 11). He stresses the essential oneness of the Father and the Son. 'We behold the Saviour's absolute deity, for it was an act of worship which was being rendered to him.'[1] Hendriksen comments, 'It is comforting to know that the Father and the Son are, indeed, *one*. We never need to be afraid that the Father is less loving than the Son or that the two work at cross-purposes.'[2]

The apostle also emphasizes the essential unity of believers: the Father is '*our* God and Father' and the Son is '*our* Lord Jesus'. Paul and his readers belonged to the same family, even though separated by many miles. They could still pray for one another. They also served the same Master—notice the title 'Lord'—though in different locations. 'God came down to be intimate with them as their gracious, loving and forgiving Father, and Jesus ascended to heaven's throne to be their sovereign Lord.'[3] Although the apostle does not explicitly mention the Holy Spirit—perhaps the word 'strengthen' (v. 13) implies his presence— it is evident, however, from Romans 8:27 that God the Holy Spirit is in full agreement with the Father and the Son.

In verse 10 Paul tells the Thessalonians, 'Night and day we pray most earnestly that we may see you again and supply what is lacking in your faith.' This, however, would not happen unless 'our Lord Jesus clear[s] the way for us to come to you' (v. 11). To 'clear the way' meant 'to remove the obstacles' that had prevented Paul going back to Thessalonica. The Amplified Bible reads, 'guide our steps to you', and is reminiscent of David's confident declaration, 'The steps of a good man are ordered by the LORD, and He delights in his way' (Ps. 37:23, NKJV). In Psalm 31:15 we read, 'My times are in your [God's] hands.' On his third missionary journey Paul visited the region of Macedonia (Acts 20:1–3) but there is no biblical evidence that he revisited Thessalonica.

Paul prays that he might 'see you again' (3:10). Do we share his yearning for the fellowship and friendship of fellow-believers? John Fawcett, in his hymn 'Blest Be the Tie That Binds', speaks of feeling pain when parted, even if only for a while, from God's people.4

Overflowing love

Timothy had spoken to Paul about the Thessalonians' 'labour prompted by love' (1:3; see also 3:6); now the apostle desires that 'the Lord [will] make your love increase and overflow for each other and for everyone else, just as ours does for you' (3:12). Love that does not 'increase' and 'overflow' soon grows cold and eventually dries up. Is Paul thinking of a river that floods the land or of a fountain that keeps flowing? The Christian's love ought to be extensive; we are to love 'each other' and 'everyone else'. The feuding Jews and Gentiles found reconciliation through Christ's cross. The 'Saviour of the world' unites believers from 'every nation, tribe, people and language' (John 4:42; Rev. 7:9).

Paul, Silas and Timothy (1:1) were living role models of how to love: 'May the Lord make your love increase and overflow … just as ours does for you.' Paul says, 'Look at us to see how to love'; would we dare say that to other Christians? Was his claim true? Yes; 1 Thessalonians chapters 1 and 2 prove that this claim was not empty boasting. The best example is, of course, the Lord Jesus Christ, who, having washed his disciples' feet, said, 'A new command I give you: Love one another. As I have loved you, so you must love one another' (John 13:34–35).

Holy living

Harmony (3:12) stimulates holiness (v. 13). Both are the result of God's power; therefore the three verses of this benediction-prayer use the word 'may', indicating that the apostle is praying that God will give his people the desire, and the ability, to live harmonious and holy lives: 'Now may our God and Father' (v. 11); 'May the Lord' (v. 12); 'May he strengthen your hearts' (v. 13). Nevertheless, God's power does not rule out human responsibility. We are responsible for living harmonious and holy lives. To fulfil this responsibility, we need God's strength (v. 13).

Paul, who sent Timothy to 'strengthen and encourage' the Thessalonians (v. 2), prays that God will also give them strength (v. 13). To 'strengthen' means to give support. Renewed strength and encouragement often come through other Christians. Believers need the support of one another.

The word 'blameless' means 'beyond reproach'; 'holy' indicates separation from sin and consecration to God (v. 13; see also 5:23). As with love, so with holiness Paul points to his own life: 'You are witnesses, and so is God, of how holy, righteous and blameless we were among you who believed' (2:10).

It is essential that we live holy lives because we must stand 'in the presence of our God and Father when our Lord Jesus comes with all his holy ones' (3:13). Then our Lord will call us to account for our loving and our living. Then he will reward those who have faithfully served him despite setbacks and discouragement. Then, at last, we will be free from sin!

Who are 'his holy ones'? Not angels, but believers ('saints', NKJV) who have gone before us to heaven. God views us as saints while we are still on earth, struggling with remaining sin, vexed by the devil and grieved by this evil world (Phil. 1:1). One day, our characters will match our title!

Notes

1 **Arthur W. Pink,** *Gleanings from Paul: The Prayers of the Apostle* (Chicago: Moody, 1967), p. 263.
2 **William Hendriksen,** *1 & 2 Thessalonians* (New Testament Commentary; London: Banner of Truth, 1972), p. 90.
3 **John MacArthur,** *1 & 2 Thessalonians*, ch. 7 (New Testament Commentary; Chicago: Moody Press, 2002; electronic edn., STEP Files © 2003, QuickVerse).
4 **John Fawcett** (1740–1817), 'Blest Be the Tie That Binds', 1782.

God is faithful (1 Thes. 5:23–24, 28)

May God himself, the God of peace, sanctify you through and through. May your whole spirit, soul and body be kept blameless at the coming of our Lord Jesus Christ. The one who calls you is faithful and he will do it ... The grace of our Lord Jesus Christ be with you.

The subject of this benediction is not primarily holiness—even though Paul uses the word 'sanctify' in verse 23; it is, rather, God's faithfulness. The focus is not on what we do but on God's power, which will bring each one of his people to sinless perfection in heaven. He 'is faithful and he will do it' (v. 24). God's faithfulness is seen against the backdrop of sanctification.

The Amplified Bible expands 'sanctify' (v. 23) as 'separate you from profane things, make you pure and wholly consecrated to God'. There are two sides to the coin of sanctification: separation from sin and consecration to God. The original Greek word means 'set apart', that is, 'kept for a special use'. God has 'set apart' Christians to love and to serve him. We belong to God because Christ purchased us with his precious blood (1 Cor. 6:19–20; 1 Peter 1:18–19). Hendriksen sums up Paul's desire for the Thessalonians: 'May this God *sanctify you*, that is, separate you from the life of sin and cause you to be dedicated to him.'[1] His summary is an excellent definition of sanctification.

How does sanctification differ from justification? Justification is God declaring us 'not guilty', once for all, at the moment of conversion. Christ was declared 'guilty' when he died in our place on the cross. On the other hand, sanctification is a gradual and progressive work of the Holy Spirit until we reach perfection in heaven. Justification is Christ's work *for* us, whereas sanctification is Christ's work *in* us.

We are justified when we believe—we come to God by faith—but faith itself is a gift from God (Eph. 2:8–9). We are sanctified—become more like Christ—as we work in harmony with the Holy Spirit. Sanctification does not cancel out human responsibility; this is why Paul's letters are full of commands about holy living. An example of this is seen in chapter 4 of this letter: 'It is God's will that you should be sanctified: that you should avoid sexual immorality; that each of you should learn to control his own body in a way that is holy and honourable … For God did not call us to be impure, but to live a holy life' (vv. 3–4, 7). We are to change our sinful conduct, but we do this only by God's power (Phil. 2:12–15).

'May God himself … sanctify you'

Paul's emphasis in verse 23 is on God's work, rather than human activity. When does God sanctify us? We are, in one sense, already sanctified! God views his people as saints, even though they are still sinners living on earth. This is the reason why Paul calls believers such as those in Ephesus and Philippi 'saints' (Eph. 1:1; Phil. 1:1). God sees our sins covered with the robe of Christ's righteousness (Isa. 61:10). 'The feeblest and least-instructed believer was as completely sanctified before God the first moment he trusted in Christ as he will be in heaven in his glorified state.'[2]

Nevertheless, sin, though it does not reign (Rom. 6:14), still remains in our hearts (Rom. 7:7–25); therefore, God works within us, through his Spirit, to change us gradually into Christ's likeness. This process will continue until 'the coming of our Lord Jesus Christ' (1 Thes. 5:23). We leave indwelling sin behind when we enter heaven at death, but when the Lord returns, our souls and bodies shall be reunited; then we shall enjoy all that Christ purchased for us by his death. Then we will be completely sanctified!

The 'God of peace'

Why does Paul address this benediction-prayer to the 'God of peace' (v. 23)? Because living peacefully with one another is an indispensable aspect of sanctification. The evidence that we are reconciled to 'the God of peace' is that we 'Live in peace with each other' (v. 13). Paul praised God for the Thessalonians' 'labour prompted by love' (1:3) and recognized their 'love [for] all the brothers throughout Macedonia', urging them to love them 'more and more' (4:10); he also prayed that God would make their love 'increase and overflow for each other' (3:12). However, some of the Thessalonians were causing problems by refusing to work because of the supposed imminent coming of Christ (4:11–12; 5:14–15; 2 Thes. 3:6–15).

In this final chapter of 1 Thessalonians, Paul commands his readers to 'respect those who work hard among you, who are over you in the Lord and who admonish you. Hold them in the highest regard in love because of their work. Live in peace with each other' (vv. 12–13). Were some of the idle members criticizing their spiritual leaders?

In the Middle East, then and now, an expression of love among believers is 'the holy kiss' (5:26; see also Rom. 16:16; 1 Cor. 16:20; 2 Cor. 13:12). Being British, I prefer a warm handshake! However we express our love for one another, it ought to be sincere and hearty.

Another facet of our love for fellow-believers is that we pray for them. In verse 17, the apostle commands his readers to 'pray continually', and in verse 25 he asks the Thessalonians to pray for Silas, Timothy and himself: 'Brothers, pray for us.' An apostle—exceptionally gifted, a worker of miracles and an author of Scripture—was not too proud to request that his spiritual children pray for him. Nor should we be!

God completes what he begins

Several times I have tried learning languages, among them Portuguese and French, and have made reasonable progress, but then the enthusiasm dwindles and what I have learnt is soon forgotten. Is God like this—

someone who starts tasks but does not finish them? Not at all! He will 'sanctify you through and through'; he will totally eradicate sin from your 'whole spirit, soul and body', so that you will stand 'blameless'—without flaw—when Christ returns (v. 23). At Christ's coming, God will sentence unbelievers to everlasting damnation; but he will spare believers from this terrible condemnation because of his sovereign grace.

I do not think that Paul is necessarily suggesting that we are made up of three parts—'spirit, soul and body'; his point is that God will completely sanctify us. If there are distinctions between these three terms, 'spirit' indicates the intellect, the 'soul' means the emotions, and the reference to 'body' is a reminder that Christians are the temple of God's Holy Spirit; this fact is a stimulus to holiness (1 Cor. 6:19–20; 2 Cor. 6:14–18).

The word 'kept' (v. 23) tells us that despite temptations and trials, in the face of opposition and persecution, and regardless of Satan's venom, God will protect his people. The emphasis of the apostle is not that Christians will be kept *until* Christ's return—though that is true—but rather that when he comes they will be fit to stand at the judgement seat because of the merits of Christ.

God is faithful

Paul highlights God's faithfulness in verse 24: 'The one who calls you is faithful and he will do it.' It is because God is faithful that he will completely sanctify his people. He never fails those who trust him; he never breaks his Word. This teaching parallels Philippians 1:6 and the doxology of Jude 24–25: '… being confident of this, that he who began a good work in you will carry it on to completion until the day of Christ Jesus'; 'To him who is able to keep you from falling and to present you before his glorious presence without fault and with great joy—to the only God our Saviour be glory, majesty, power and authority, through Jesus Christ our Lord, before all ages, now and for evermore! Amen.' What matters is not our weak hold on God, but his grasp of us!

Paul mentions in verse 24 God's call: this is the irresistible call of the Holy Spirit 'to live a holy life' now (4:7) and to enter 'his kingdom and glory' later (2:12; 2 Thes. 2:14). Those whom God calls are 'justified' and 'glorified' (Rom. 8:30). Paul uses the past tense for future glorification because there is no one and nothing that can frustrate God's eternal decree to completely save all his elect.

Grace

So Paul ends this letter with the familiar words that occur, with slight variations, near the end of all his letters (v. 28; see also 2 Thes. 3:18). As ever, he points us to the unmerited grace of the matchless Saviour: 'The grace of our Lord Jesus Christ be with you.'

Notes

1 **William Hendriksen,** *1 & 2 Thessalonians* (New Testament Commentary; London: Banner of Truth, 1972), p. 141.

2 **Arthur W. Pink,** *Gleanings from Paul: The Prayers of the Apostle* (Chicago: Moody, 1967), p. 274.

Eternal encouragement (2 Thes. 2:16–17)

May our Lord Jesus Christ himself and God our Father, who loved us and by his grace gave us eternal encouragement and good hope, encourage your hearts and strengthen you in every good deed and word.

I magine Paul as an old man looking back on his life. Which events would he recall? He would certainly never forget his three weeks' visit to Thessalonica in AD 50. In less than a month Paul's powerful preaching gave birth to a church. Then the Jews called the 'rent-a-mob' office to hire a rabble that chased Paul out of the city. The apostle barely escaped with his life.

A year later Paul wrote two letters— two of his earliest letters—to this growing church in northern Greece. What does the apostle tell this young church? He writes about the future. The future is both bright and bleak. It is bright because Christ is coming, but bleak because 'the man of lawlessness' (2 Thes. 2:3), the Antichrist, is also coming. Therefore, Paul writes to encourage the church by reminding them of two great facts for which he thanks God: God has chosen them and God has called them (2:13–14). These two truths lead to the twofold appeal of verse 15: 'So then, brothers, stand firm and hold to the teachings we passed on to you'; then follows Paul's benediction in verses 16–17. This benediction is one of four prayers in his second letter to the Thessalonians (1:11–12; 2:16–17; 3:5, 16).

Father, Son and Spirit

We have already noted in previous chapters that several benedictions have a Trinitarian structure; this benediction provides a further example. Paul prays to 'our Lord Jesus Christ himself and God our Father' (v. 16). God the Father and God the Son work with God the Holy Spirit (though he is not explicitly mentioned) to save those whom God has chosen (v. 13). The apostle has no hesitation in linking the Father and the Son; both are God and both are worthy of adoration. Why is the Son placed before the Father? Because we come to God through Christ. It is not at the throne of sovereignty, but at the cross of dying love, that our spiritual life dates its birth.

God the Son

Paul gives God the Son his full title: 'Lord Jesus Christ' (v. 16). He is the Lord who commands obedience, and Jesus, the unique Saviour who calls us to repentance and shows us mercy. The name Jesus means Saviour (Matt. 1:21). The title 'Christ' is the Greek equivalent of the Hebrew 'Messiah' and means 'anointed'. He came, in fulfilment of the Old Testament Scriptures, as the Prophet, Priest and King, anointed at his baptism by the Holy Spirit for his ministry (Matt. 3:13–17).

Christ becomes '*our* Lord Jesus Christ' when we trust him for salvation. This personal possession of Christ gives us boldness to approach God and confidence as we serve him. God accepts all who come to him through Christ (Heb. 4:14–16; 10:19–22).

What is the significance of the emphatic pronoun 'himself'? It is Christ—not a proxy—who gives us 'eternal encouragement and good hope'. Just as it is the mother, rather than the competent childminder, who gives her sick child cuddles, so it is Christ himself who gives comfort and strength to his children in times of danger and distress. To change the metaphor, soldiers on the battlefield are encouraged when they see their commander fighting alongside them.

God the Father

We pray to 'God our Father, who loved us' (v. 16). This love is more than pity. We may feel pity towards someone we do not like. This love is more than mere kindness. God loves us as a *father*. It is usual for fathers and mothers to love their children as they love themselves; the children are part of themselves. Likewise, God the Father feels an intense love for his children. His love is greater than that of human parents. Psalm 103:13–14 and Isaiah 49:15 are helpful here:

As a father has compassion on his children,
so the LORD has compassion on those who fear him;
for he knows how we are formed,
he remembers that we are dust.

Can a mother forget the baby at her breast
and have no compassion on the child she has borne?
Though she may forget,
I will not forget you!

In these verses God compares himself to an understanding, caring father and contrasts himself with a mother who rejects her newborn baby. A realization of the Father's love 'will keep our hearts warm and our affections fresh towards God'.[1]

God our Father gives his children 'eternal encouragement and good hope' (2 Thes. 2:16). The Thessalonians were in need of encouragement and hope because of bereavement (1 Thes. 4:13), persecution (2 Thes. 1:4) and Paul's prediction about 'the man of lawlessness' (2 Thes. 2:1–12).

ENCOURAGEMENT

Let us look more closely at the terms used by Paul in verse 16. The word 'encouragement' ('consolation', NKJV) comes from a Greek word that is difficult to translate into English. It has the same root as the description of the Holy Spirit in John 14:16—'Counsellor' ('Comforter', KJV; 'Helper', NKJV/ESV)—and the title of Christ in 1 John 2:1: 'Advocate' (NKJV). The NIV translates the word behind 'Advocate' as 'one who speaks to the Father in our defence'. The meaning of this word is 'come alongside'. God comes to our side in our sinfulness and in our sorrow. He comes not just to soothe, but also to give us strength to keep going when life is tough.

This encouragement is undeserved; it comes to us 'by his grace'. It is also 'eternal', in contrast to the fleeting and superficial comforts which this world offers (e.g. drink, drugs). This encouragement often comes through the presence and the prayers of fellow-believers. Paul sent Tychicus to the Colossians 'that he may encourage your hearts' (Col. 4:7–8). The apostle prays in this benediction that Christ and God the Father will 'encourage your hearts' (2 Thes. 2:17).

Why does God give encouragement? To make us strong for service! Look again at verses 16–17: 'May our Lord ... and God our Father ... encourage your hearts and strengthen you in every good deed and word.' We must not think of God's encouragement and comfort as a painkiller, but rather as a renewing of energy for service and sanctification.

Thomas Manton compares the effect of God's comfort to the difference between a shower and the dew: 'God's comfort is like a soaking shower that goes to the root and refreshes the plants of the earth, rather than a morning dew that wets only the surface. Other comforts tickle the senses and refresh the outward man, but this penetrates the heart.'[2]

Paul prays that God will strengthen his people for 'every good deed and word'. It is those who are busy in God's work who will be spiritually strong. How better could we respond to God's love and grace than by serving him? God's love evokes the best in us, just as a master musician brings out melodies from an instrument that inferior players fail to produce.

HOPE

The 'good hope' of verse 16 is confidence in God's promises. God never breaks his Word. Paul wrote about this hope in his short letter to Titus, who was encouraging believers in Crete: '... the faith of God's elect and the knowledge of the truth that leads to godliness—a faith and knowledge resting on the hope of eternal life, which God, who does not lie, promised before the beginning of time' (Titus 1:1–2). In the next chapter, Paul wrote that believers 'wait for the blessed hope—the glorious appearing of our great God and Saviour, Jesus Christ' (Titus 2:13). This hope enables Christians to live now on earth, even in the most appalling circumstances.

The story is told of Portuguese explorers sailing south who found the seas so stormy around the southern part of Africa that they named it the Cape of Storms. Later, when more experienced navigators rounded the same coastline, they renamed it the Cape of Good Hope.[3] God's help transforms many rough capes of storms into capes of good hope.

Notes

1 **Arthur W. Pink,** *Gleanings from Paul: The Prayers of the Apostle* (Chicago: Moody, 1967), p. 309.

2 **Thomas Manton,** *The Complete Works of Thomas Manton*, vol. iii (London: James Nisbet & Co., 1871), p. 169.

3 From **C. H. Spurgeon,** 'Memory: The Handmaid of Hope', Sermon 654, in *The Metropolitan Tabernacle Pulpit*, vol. xi (1865; electronic edn., AGES). Spurgeon's sermons are available online at www.spurgeon.org. In 2009 Day One published **Terence Peter Crosby,** *C. H. Spurgeon's Sermons beyond Volume 63*. For an excellent summary of Spurgeon's life, read **Clive Anderson,** *Travel with C. H. Spurgeon: In the Footsteps of the Prince of Preachers* (Leominster: Day One, 2002).

The Lord of peace
(2 Thes. 3:5, 16–18)

May the Lord direct your hearts into God's love and Christ's perseverance … Now may the Lord of peace himself give you peace at all times and in every way. The Lord be with all of you. I, Paul, write this greeting in my own hand, which is the distinguishing mark in all my letters. This is how I write. The grace of our Lord Jesus Christ be with you all.

P aul writes these benedictions in the context of diligent believers serving the Lord (3:1), wicked men opposing the gospel (v. 2) and lazy Christians causing trouble within the church (vv. 6–14). Only the Lord of peace can give peace when his people face the hatred of the ungodly. He alone can restore peace in divided churches.

Who is 'the Lord' of whom Paul writes in verses 5 and 16? Paul answers that question when he says he prays to 'our *Lord* Jesus Christ' (2:16, emphasis added) and commends the Thessalonians to 'the grace of our *Lord* Jesus Christ' (3:18). Christ gives his people peace. However, we could also say that it is the triune God—Father, Son and Holy Spirit—who bestows peace; peace flows from each Person of the Trinity (Heb. 13:20; Gal. 5:22; Isa. 9:6).

Christ's faithfulness

The Lord who directs his people (v. 5) is faithful; he 'will strengthen and protect' them 'from the evil one' (v. 3). Paul knew from his own experience that Christ gives strength to the weak. He prayed three times for God to take away his 'thorn in the flesh' (probably a physical

The Lord of peace (2 Thes. 3:5, 16–18)

disability), but the Lord said to him, 'My grace is sufficient for you, for my power is made perfect in weakness.' It was through bearing this 'thorn' that Paul learnt that 'when I am weak, then I am strong' (2 Cor. 12:7–10). The apostle dated this traumatic incident to 'fourteen years' before his second letter to the Corinthians (2 Cor. 12:2)—this would take us back to the time before he wrote his two letters to the Thessalonians. I am assuming that the Thessalonian letters were written about AD 51 and that he penned the Corinthian letters about AD 56/57.

The word 'protect' (v. 3) brings to mind the picture of a city that is being attacked. The mighty Lord defends his church, which is often pictured in Scripture as a city. We have an example of this in Hebrews 12:22–23, where we read that believers have come—in this present life—to 'Mount Zion, to the heavenly Jerusalem, the city of the living God … to the church of the firstborn, whose names are written in heaven'. Christ builds his church, and the gates of Hades (that is, hell—Satan and demons) will not destroy it (Matt. 16:18).

The 'evil one' (v. 3) is not difficult to identify. He is 'The great dragon … that ancient serpent called the devil, or Satan, who leads the whole world astray … who accuses them [Christians] before our God day and night'. Christians overcome him 'by the blood of the Lamb [Christ] and by the word of their testimony' (Rev. 12:9–11). Christ died to conquer Satan; therefore, we may resist him and see him flee (Col. 2:15; James 4:7). The wise Christian prays, 'And lead us not into temptation, but deliver us from the evil one' (Matt. 6:13).

The outcome of Christ's strengthening and protecting is that the believer continues to obey God (v. 4). God's Word came to the Thessalonians in Paul's commands. God's Word comes to us now in the Bible. Obedience is the evidence, and the hallmark, of genuine faith. The apostle attests that 'not everyone has faith' (v. 2), but he has 'confidence in the Lord' that the Thessalonians are true Christians (v. 4). The faithful God will never fail them. It is by his power that they obey his commands.

Now we come to the apostle's benediction in verse 5. The word translated 'direct' (rendered in 1 Thes. 3:11 as 'clear the way') means 'make straight' and indicates removing obstacles from the road. Paul prays that the Lord will direct his readers into God's love.

Should we understand 'God's love' objectively (his love for us) or subjectively (our love for him)? Perhaps the apostle deliberately used some ambiguity so that we may take his words either way. He desired that his readers 'go down the pathway deeper and deeper into God's love for them, which in turn would cause them to love him more and more'.[1]

Paul desires that the Thessalonians will also go deeper into 'Christ's perseverance' ('patience', NKJV). Again, there is some ambiguity in the term used. MacArthur explains, 'Paul wanted the Thessalonians to increasingly understand how patient Christ was with their sins, problems, and struggles and to understand better His own endurance in trials.'[2] Christ's perseverance provides the model, and the motivation, for the Christian's perseverance (compare Heb. 12:1–3).

Christ's peace

The second benediction in 2 Thessalonians 3 begins in verse 16: 'Now may the Lord of peace himself give you peace at all times and in every way. The Lord be with all of you.' Through Christ, we have peace *with* God (Rom. 5:1) and we know the peace *of* God (Phil. 4:7). The first is reconciliation. We are reconciled to the holy God because Christ shed his blood on the cross (Col. 1:20). The second is calmly trusting God in times of trouble. The apostle wrote about the peace of God and commanded the Philippians to pray and to praise while he was locked in a Roman prison (Phil. 1:13; 4:4–7). I think that it is peace in pain and problems that is uppermost in Paul's mind in this benediction.

Christ's peace was experienced by the wives of the five American missionaries speared to death by the Auca Indians on 8 January 1956.

They said, 'The Lord has closed our hearts to grief and hysteria, and filled us with his perfect peace.' One of the wives, Elisabeth Elliot, together with these other women, began work among the murderers of their husbands and saw many of them converted to Christ.[3] It is not wrong to grieve—Jesus wept at the grave of his close friend, Lazarus (John 11:35)—but God gave these bereaved women an extraordinary sense of his peace.

Who were these courageous martyred missionaries? Their names were Jim Elliot, Pete Fleming, Ed McCully, Nate Saint and Roger Youderian. Jim Elliot's words are often quoted: 'He is no fool who gives what he cannot keep to gain that which he cannot lose.' What is not so well known is that he based this saying on the words of Philip Henry, father of the famous eighteenth-century pastor and Bible commentator Matthew Henry.[4]

Edward Kulczyki, who was a member of Mirfield Evangelical Church, West Yorkshire, also knew God's peace as he faced imminent death. In his testimony, published in *Grace Magazine* in January 2010, he said, 'I am now fifty-five and have a short time left with cancer in the bowel, liver and lung. Death is on the horizon, but I can depart this world in the sure knowledge that I am forgiven and that my heavenly Father has the door wide open to receive me.' In fact, by the time of publication, Edward had already entered that door.[5]

To return to 2 Thessalonians 3:16, note the word 'himself'. Peace does not come from sinless angels, departed Christians or even from godly spiritual leaders, but from Christ alone. Paul, though an apostle, cannot confer this peace, but he can pray for Christ to give it to the Thessalonians.

When do we need Christ's peace? Paul tells us: 'at all times and in every way'. The Amplified Bible expands these words to 'at all times and in all ways [under all circumstances and conditions, whatever comes]'.

Christ's presence

Paul prays, 'The Lord be with all of you' (v. 16). Leon Morris comments, 'The Christian's peace is the presence of the Lord.'[6] Spurgeon, preaching from 2 Thessalonians 3:16, alluded to Christ restoring peace to the stormy Sea of Galilee (Mark 4:35–41):

If he is present you may enjoy peace. Let the sea rage and let every timber of the ship be strained … let her leak till between each timber there yawns a hungry mouth to swallow you up … yet when Christ arises he will rebuke the winds and the waves, and there will be great calm. 'It is I, be not afraid' is enough to create peace at once.[7]

The 'all' in verse 16 includes the persecuted (1 Thes. 2:14), the mourners (4:13), the timid and the weak (5:14), spiritual leaders (5:12–13) and even the idle 'busybodies' (2 Thes. 3:11). Paul wanted every member of the church at Thessalonica to 'Live in peace with each other' (1 Thes. 5:13).

Persecution compelled Paul to leave Thessalonica in a hurry, but Christ was still with his people; he would never leave them. Neither will he leave us, whatever happens in our lives. We rest on God's unbreakable promise: 'He [God] Himself has said, I will not in any way fail you nor give you up nor leave you without support. [I will] not, [I will] not, [I will] not in any degree leave you helpless, nor forsake you, nor let [you] down (relax My hold on you)! [Assuredly not!]' (Heb. 13:5, Amplified Bible).

Before we consider the third blessing that Paul desired for the Thessalonians, look at verse 17. Paul, who dictated this letter, perhaps to Timothy or Silas (1:1), took the pen to add a few words in his own handwriting. Why did the apostle call special attention to the authenticity of this letter? For two reasons: firstly, to enforce obedience from rebellious church members (v. 12); and, secondly, to prevent the circulation of spurious letters (2:2).

Christ's grace

Peace (v. 16) and grace (v. 18) are like inseparable twins in Paul's letters. There is no peace without grace, and no grace without peace. The apostle could not desire for the Thessalonians anything more precious than Christ's peace and Christ's grace. Neither can we ask for one another any blessings more important than these.

The benediction of verse 18 is the same as that which concludes the first letter (1 Thes. 5:28), except for the word 'all'. 'Was this word added in order to make sure that the individuals who had received a rebuke would feel that, in Paul's great and loving heart, there was room even for them?'[8]

Notes

1 **John MacArthur,** *1 & 2 Thessalonians*, ch. 25 (New Testament Commentary; Chicago: Moody Press, 2002; electronic edn., STEP Files © 2003, QuickVerse).

2 Ibid.

3 The story of their martyrdom is told in **Elisabeth Elliot,** *Through Gates of Splendor* (New York: Harper, 1957).

4 **Rev. Matthew Henry, V. D. M.,** *The Life of the Rev. Philip Henry, A. M., with Funeral Sermons for Mr. and Mrs. Henry* (Chester, 1711–1712; repr. London: J. B. Williams, 1825; now digitized by Google at www.books.google.com). The quote, 'He is no fool who parts with that which he cannot keep, when he is sure to be recompensed with that which he cannot lose', can be found on p. 35.

5 *Grace Magazine*, www.gracemagazine.org.uk.

6 **Leon Morris,** *1 & 2 Thessalonians* (Tyndale New Testament Commentary; London: Tyndale Press, 1956), p. 151.

7 **C. H. Spurgeon,** 'The Jewel of Peace', Sermon 1343, in *The Metropolitan Tabernacle Pulpit*, vol. xxiii, 1877 (electronic edn., AGES).

8 **William Hendriksen,** *1 & 2 Thessalonians* (New Testament Commentary; London: Banner of Truth, 1972), p. 209.

The eternal King
(1 Tim. 1:17; 6:15–16, 21)

Now to the King eternal, immortal, invisible, the only God, be honour and glory for ever and ever. Amen …

… God, the blessed and only Ruler, the King of kings and Lord of lords, who alone is immortal and who lives in unapproachable light, whom no one has seen or can see. To him be honour and might for ever. Amen … Grace be with you.

Both these benedictions flow from Paul's mentions of Christ's comings: his first coming, mentioned in 1 Timothy 1 (v. 15); and his second coming, mentioned in 1 Timothy 6 (v. 14). He came to save sinners such as Paul; he is coming to assess the lives of saints. Because he is coming, we are to be 'without spot or blame' (6:14): his coming motivates holy living.

The term 'spot' brings to mind Peter's description of Christ as a lamb without 'blemish and without spot' (1 Peter 1:19, NKJV). He was 'without blemish or defect' (NIV). On earth, we aim to be like Christ; in heaven we shall be like him—'a radiant church, without stain ['spot', NKJV] or wrinkle or any other blemish, but holy and blameless' (Eph. 5:27). The word 'blame' means 'beyond reproach' (compare 1 Tim. 3:2, 10).

In chapter 1, Paul's statements about the ministry to which God had called him and the mercy that God had shown him (1:12–16) overflow into praise of the Monarch whom he adored (v. 17). Does God need our praise? Not at all! So why offer him praise? 'Praise is offered to God not because he needs it but because he is entitled to it and because it is a testimony to our reverence, faith and love for him.'[1]

The focus of both doxologies is God: what God is like and how we ought to praise him.

God is sovereign

God is 'the King' (1:17); he is the 'Ruler, the King of kings and Lord of lords' (6:15). God is the Sovereign who rules the entire universe. He is the King who plans everything. He governs all the activities of the human race. Kings and lords—human rulers—derive their authority from him and are accountable to him.

These benedictions of Paul the apostle parallel the praise of Daniel the prophet:

Then Daniel praised the God of heaven and said:
'Praise be to the name of God for ever and ever;
    wisdom and power are his.
He changes times and seasons;
    he sets up kings and deposes them.
He gives wisdom to the wise
    and knowledge to the discerning.
He reveals deep and hidden things;
    he knows what lies in darkness,
    and light dwells with him.
I thank and praise you, O God of my fathers;
    you have given me wisdom and power,
you have made known to me what we asked of you,
    you have made known to us the dream of the king.'   (Dan. 2:19–23)

Later, Nebuchadnezzar expressed similar thoughts to those of Daniel:

At the end of that time, I, Nebuchadnezzar, raised my eyes towards heaven, and my sanity was restored. Then I praised the Most High; I honoured and glorified him who lives for ever.

His dominion is an eternal dominion;
>   his kingdom endures from generation to generation.
All the peoples of the earth
>   are regarded as nothing.
He does as he pleases
>   with the powers of heaven
>   and the peoples of the earth.
No one can hold back his hand
>   or say to him: 'What have you done?' (Dan. 4:34–35)

Paul's description of God—'the King of kings and Lord of lords' (6:15)—is used of Christ twice in the book of Revelation: 'The Lamb ... is the Lord of lords and King of Kings' (17:14); 'On his robe and on his thigh he has this name written: KING OF KINGS AND LORD OF LORDS' (19:16).

God is eternal

God the King is 'eternal': he is without beginning or end. He is the King who cannot die; no enemy can depose or defeat him. His kingdom is everlasting. His care of his people is never-ending and unchanging.

Consider the psalmist's declaration of God's eternity:

In the beginning you laid the foundations of the earth,
>   and the heavens are the work of your hands.
They will perish, but you remain;
>   they will all wear out like a garment.
Like clothing you will change them
>   and they will be discarded.

But you remain the same,

> and your years will never end. (Ps. 102:25–27)

The writer to the Hebrews quoted these words to prove that Christ is eternal and unchanging (Heb. 1:10–12).

God is immortal

He is 'immortal' (1:17); he 'alone is immortal' (6:16). This implies more than endless existence. Paul's point is that God does not derive his life from something or someone else: he has always existed; he is uncreated. He created—and was the source of life in—the universe (Gen. 1:1; John 1:1–4). The immortal God gives 'life and immortality' to believers (2 Tim. 1:10). Every person has a soul that will never die; however, there is a vast difference between the never-ending existence of the damned in hell and the everlasting joy of believers in heaven.

God gives believers eternal life; therefore, they will never perish (John 3:16; 10:28–29). God has also prepared for them 'an inheritance that can never perish, spoil or fade'. This inheritance is 'kept in heaven', and the heirs are kept 'by God's power' (1 Peter 1:4–5). When Christ comes, the mortal and perishable bodies of Christians will be changed into immortal and imperishable bodies (1 Cor. 15:51–57).

What is the difference between the immortality of God and the immortality of believers? 'While the believer has received immortality, as one receives a drink of water from a fountain, God has it. It belongs to his very being. He is himself the Fountain.'[2]

God is invisible

The 'King eternal' is 'invisible' (1:17); God 'lives in unapproachable light' and 'no one has seen or can see' him (6:16). We cannot see God because he is a spirit who has no body. Talking to a woman in Samaria Jesus said, 'God is spirit, and his worshippers must worship in spirit and in truth' (John 4:24). This woman needed to grasp that the condition of the heart was more important than the place where she worshipped (vv. 19–23). God looks for sincerity and truthfulness from those who worship him.

The second of the Ten Commandments (Exod. 20:4–5) forbids the use of images and pictures in worship because we do not know what God looks like. Images always become the objects of worship rather than aids to worship. They turn our focus away from the invisible God to a visible representation.

Hendriksen explains why we cannot approach the invisible God of light: 'This light is like the sun. We need it to see by, yet we cannot look into it, for it is too intensely brilliant. In that sense, God dwells in light unapproachable.'[3] This is why, when Moses asked to see God's glory, God said, '… you cannot see my face, for no one may see me and live.' God graciously showed Moses his hand and his back, but not his face (Exod. 33:18–23).

How could Moses see the hand and back of God who has no physical body? This was a theophany—an appearance of God the Son before his incarnation at Bethlehem.[4] Before the incarnation Christ sometimes appeared in what *looked like* a human body; at the incarnation, he took a real human body with a real human nature. A theophany was a temporary appearance; the incarnation was permanent. Even now in heaven, Christ has a real human nature and therefore feels for us when we suffer (Heb. 4:14–16).[5]

Is it possible to know the invisible God? Yes! We see God in Christ. The apostle John, alluding to God's words to Moses, wrote, 'No one has seen God at any time. The only begotten Son, who is in the bosom of the Father, He has declared Him' (John 1:18, NKJV). The eternal and uncreated Son, who lived in close fellowship with his Father, stepped out of eternity into time to show us God. To see Christ is to see God (John 14:8–11). He is one with the Father (John 10:30). The apostle Paul stated that 'He [Christ] is the image of the invisible God' (Col. 1:15; see also Heb. 1:3). It is through Christ, and because of Christ, that God pardons penitent sinners.

One day, we will see God! Job, who probably lived around the time of Abraham, about 2,000 years before Christ, affirmed,

I know that my Redeemer lives,
> and that in the end he will stand upon the earth.

And after my skin has been destroyed,
> yet in my flesh I will see God;

I myself will see him
> with my own eyes—I, and not another.
> How my heart yearns within me!   (Job 19:25–27; compare Matt. 5:8; 1 John 3:2)

God is blessed

Paul calls God 'the blessed and only Ruler' (6:15). 'Blessed' indicates that God is successful in all that he does; his plans are always accomplished. He is perfectly happy and content. He gives this blessedness to his children; they are those in whom he delights and to whom he gives lasting joy, peace, satisfaction and contentment (Matt. 5:1–12). He will give his people 'eternal pleasures' at his 'right hand' (Ps. 16:11).

God is unique

There is only one God: he is 'the only God' (1:17), the 'only Ruler' (6:15). He is completely different from Allah, the god of the Muslims, and the assortment of gods of Hinduism. There are no other gods. In a world in which people venerated many gods, the Hebrew prophet Isaiah wrote,

This is what the LORD says—
> Israel's King and Redeemer, the Lord Almighty:

I am the first and I am the last;

apart from me there is no God.

Who then is like me? Let him proclaim it.

Let him declare and lay out before me …

Do not tremble, do not be afraid …

You are my witnesses. Is there any God besides me?

No, there is no other Rock; I know not one.   (Isa. 44:6–8)

Isaiah derided those who worshipped gods they had made with their own hands (vv. 9–20).

How may we know 'the only God'? Through the only Saviour, the Lord Jesus Christ, who said, 'I am the way and the truth and the life. No one comes to the Father except through me' (John 14:6). Paul affirmed that 'there is one God and one mediator between God and men, the man Christ Jesus, who gave himself as a ransom for all men' (1 Tim. 2:5–6). The word 'ransom' denotes the costly price he paid to deliver us from sin's power.

There is some variation in the different Bible translations for the phrase 'the only God' at 1:17; for example, 'God who alone is wise' (NKJV). This rendering parallels Paul's doxology in Romans 11:33: 'Oh, the depth of the riches of the wisdom and knowledge of God! How unsearchable his judgements, and his paths beyond tracing out!' The wise God knows and sees everything—past, present and future. The wise God works all things for good in the lives of his people (Rom. 8:28). The wise God generously gives wisdom to those who ask him (James 1:5).

God deserves honour, glory and might

A realization that God is sovereign, eternal, immortal, invisible, blessed and unique will lead to the desire that his honour, glory and might will be extolled for ever (1:17; 6:16). We honour God as we 'fight the good fight, holding on to faith and a good conscience' (1:18–19).

A young man's conversion

Jonathan, aged eighteen, the son of a godly pastor in eighteenth-century New England, was reading his Bible one day. As he read Paul's first letter to Timothy, the words seemed to leap off the page: 'Now to the King eternal, immortal, invisible, the only God, be honour and glory for ever and ever. Amen.' The story is better told in his own words:

As I read these words there came into my soul ... a sense of the glory of the Divine Being; a new sense, quite different from anything I ever experienced before ... I thought ... how excellent a Being that was, and how happy I should be, if indeed I might enjoy that God, and be rapt up in him in heaven and be ... swallowed up forever in him! I kept saying, and, as it were, singing over these words of Scripture to myself ... I began to have a new kind of apprehension and ideas about Christ, and the work of redemption, and the glorious way of salvation by him ... My mind was greatly engaged to spend time in reading and meditating on Christ, on the beauty and excellency of his person, and the lovely way of salvation by free grace in him.

Jonathan Edwards, who served as pastor of a church in Northampton, Massachusetts, for twenty-three years, never lost the amazement that he felt at his conversion through reading Paul's benediction in 1 Timothy 1:17.[6]

Grace

Paul concludes both his letters to Timothy with two succinct benedictions: 'Grace be with you' (1 Tim. 6:21) and 'The Lord be with your spirit. Grace be with you' (2 Tim. 4:22). The apostle uses the same benediction in his letter to Titus: 'Grace be with you all' (Titus 3:15). The word 'all' indicates that Titus was to share Paul's letter with the believers on the island of Crete. God's grace, which saved Timothy and Titus, would keep them until the Saviour's reappearing (2 Tim. 4:8; Titus 2:11–14).

Chapter 18

Notes

1 **Arthur W. Pink,** *Gleanings from Paul: The Prayers of the Apostle* (Chicago: Moody, 1967), p. 340.
2 **William Hendriksen,** *1 & 2 Timothy and Titus* (New Testament Commentary; London: Banner of Truth, 1960), p. 208.
3 Ibid.
4 See 'Appendix 2: Old Testament Appearances of God—Theophanies', in my book *Christ in Exodus* (London: Grace Publications, 2010), pp. 148–150.
5 See **Robert Sheehan,** *The Word of Truth* (Darlington: Evangelical Press, 1998), pp. 40–47. Sheehan explains how God revealed himself in the Old Testament, including the pre-incarnate appearances of Christ—theophanies.
6 Quoted in **Iain Murray,** *Jonathan Edwards: A New Biography* (Edinburgh: Banner of Truth, 1987), pp. 35–36.

The almighty Deliverer (2 Tim. 4:18, 22)

The Lord will rescue me from every evil attack and will bring me safely to his heavenly kingdom. To him be glory for ever and ever. Amen ... The Lord be with your spirit. Grace be with you.

Chained in a Roman cell, alone with Luke, the historian and doctor (4:11; Luke 1:1–4; Col. 4:14), Paul, now an old man (Philem. 9), is anxious to see his young assistant, Timothy.

'Do your best to come to me quickly ... Do your best to get here before winter,' he writes (vv. 9, 21), because he knows that time is running out— soon he will die a martyr's death. 'Old' for Paul, worn out by his sufferings (2:8–10; 2 Cor. 11:23–30), was probably about sixty, several years older than the faithful Timothy, who was busy caring for the church at Ephesus.

Would the apostle's spiritual son (1:2) or the executioner arrive first in Paul's cell? Tough times were ahead (3:1–13), so the apostle urged Timothy to 'Fight the good fight of the faith' (1 Tim. 6:12) and to 'Endure hardship with us like a good soldier of Christ Jesus' (2 Tim. 2:3). The old warrior looked back and wrote truthfully, 'I have fought the good fight, I have finished the race. I have kept the faith' (4:7). Unrighteous judges were about to condemn him to death, but the righteous Judge would award him 'a crown of righteousness' (4:8). This was not a fading laurel wreath, such as the Olympic athlete received, but an eternal inheritance that would never perish, spoil or fade (1 Peter 1:4).

The past

Paul praises God (4:18) even when abandoned by human friends. He writes, 'At my first defence, no one came to my support, but everyone deserted me'; then he graciously adds, 'May it not be held against them' (v. 16). The apostle's graciousness displayed his own teaching about love in 1 Corinthians 13.

We see another expression of Paul's forgiving attitude in verse 11: 'Get Mark and bring him with you, because he is helpful to me in my ministry.' This was John Mark, the author of the Gospel that bears his name. Mark had left the apostle during his first missionary journey, so that Paul refused to take him a second time. This caused a rift between Paul and Mark's uncle, Barnabas (Acts 13:5, 13; 15:36–40). Since then, Mark had proved useful to Paul. God does not desert the deserters! He welcomes the penitent backslider. God's grace had united the two men once again.

Why had no one supported Paul? Crescens was serving God in Galatia, and Titus was in Dalmatia, 'a Roman province on the [east] coast of the Adriatic Sea, just [north] of Macedonia'.[1] Present-day Dalmatia is in Croatia, one of the regions of the former Yugoslavia. Tychicus had gone to Ephesus, presumably to make it possible for Timothy to travel to Paul. Where was Luke at the time of Paul's first trial? We don't know, but it appears that he was unable to speak in defence of his friend. Speaking against Paul was probably 'Alexander the metalworker [who] did me a great deal of harm'. Without malice, Paul declares, 'The Lord will repay him for what he has done' (v. 14).

Can we imagine tears in Paul's eyes as he remembers Demas, who, because he 'loved this world', had forsaken him and, more seriously, had deserted Christ (v. 10)? 'The world of suffering for the sake of Christ was obviously too much for him. He preferred the world of ease and pleasure.'[2] Do we love Christ more than this world (Rom. 12:1–2; 1 John 2:15–17)?

Paul could testify that, in contrast to those who had deserted him, '…

the Lord stood at my side and gave me strength, so that through me the message might be fully proclaimed and all the Gentiles might hear it. And I was delivered from the lion's mouth' (v. 17). Christ's presence filled Paul with praise as he anticipated imminent death.

The 'Lord stood at [Paul's] side' when he was rescued by Roman soldiers from the violent arguing of the Sadducees and Pharisees. On that occasion, the Lord spoke in a dream to the apostle: 'Take courage! As you have testified about me in Jerusalem, so you must also testify in Rome' (Acts 23:9–11). Paul was now in Rome; the Lord had kept his word.

The same Lord stood at the side of three brave Jews—Shadrach, Meshach and Abednego—in 'the furnace heated seven times hotter than usual', because they refused to bow before the huge golden image of Nebuchadnezzar, the Babylonian king (Dan. 3:19–23). Later, the king saw a fourth person in the flames; it was 'the Son of God' (v. 25, NKJV) who walked with them! This was a theophany: a preincarnate appearance of Christ.[3] When they were released the king saw 'that the fire had not harmed their bodies, nor was a hair of their heads singed; their robes were not scorched, and there was no smell of fire on them' (vv. 26–27).

The Lord stood at the side of Paul to give him boldness, so that 'the message might be fully proclaimed and all the Gentiles might hear it' (2 Tim. 4:17). Some of these Gentiles were his judges, who might have included Nero himself. At the time of his first Roman imprisonment Paul had asked the Ephesians to 'Pray … that whenever I open my mouth, words may be given me so that I will fearlessly make known the mystery of the gospel' (Eph. 6:19). God had answered their prayers. We too ought to pray for courage to speak about Christ to our family and friends.

Who was the lion, from whose mouth Paul was delivered (v. 17)? As a Roman citizen, Paul could not be thrown to the lions, so he must have been speaking metaphorically. He was probably referring to the emperor Nero, though he may have had in mind Satan, whom Peter compared to 'a roaring lion' (1 Peter 5:8). John Calvin wrote that Paul was delivered 'out of the jaws of death'.4

God closed the mouths of lions when Daniel was thrown by Darius into their den. 'Pray only to me for a month,' demanded the monarch (Dan. 6:7). Daniel, now in his eighties, continued to pray to God three times each day, just as he had done for years—and he was thrown to the lions. The next morning, Daniel told the anxious king, 'My God sent his angel, and he shut the mouths of the lions. They have not hurt me, because I was found innocent in his sight. Nor have I ever done any wrong before you, O king' (v. 21).

The future

Paul turns his thoughts from the past—'I *was* delivered' (vv. 16–17)—to the future—'The Lord *will* rescue me' (v. 18, emphasis added). 'In the past he had been rescued *from* death. Now he will be rescued *by means of* death. In neither case does his soul perish. He is never separated from the love of God in Christ.'5

The apostle Paul expects, at death, to enter immediately into Christ's 'heavenly kingdom' (v. 18). To be 'away from the body' is to be 'at home with the Lord', waiting 'to be clothed with our heavenly dwelling' (see 2 Cor. 5:1–10); this is the resurrection body of which Paul writes in 1 Corinthians 15.

Death holds no fear for Paul; he describes dying as 'my departure' (v. 6), a word that in the original Greek was used of untying a boat from its moorings. At the moment of death the boat of life sets sail on its last journey towards the port of heaven.

Christ will bring every one of his dying people 'safely to his heavenly kingdom' (v. 18). No one will be lost on the way to that kingdom. All for whom the Saviour died will enter heaven. He says to each dying saint, '... today you will be with me in paradise' (Luke 23:43). The word 'paradise' depicts heaven as a beautiful garden. Death is to be 'with me'—

consciously in the presence of Christ. The risen Lord who stood to receive the martyr Stephen will welcome each believer into heaven (Acts 7:54–56).

Is it any wonder that at the anticipation of the 'heavenly kingdom' Paul bursts into a doxology? 'To him be glory for ever and ever. Amen' (v. 18). The 'Amen' tells us that the 'heavenly kingdom' is what the apostle eagerly desires. It is also a declaration that he, and all believers, will enter Christ's kingdom.

The present

Paul knows that execution will come shortly. Meanwhile, he asks Timothy to bring his cloak, to keep him warm in winter, and 'my scrolls, especially the parchments' (v. 13). Ligon Duncan, preaching at a pastors' conference in Chicago in April 2009, remarked, 'If Paul was learning, reading, studying, and writing to the very end, surely we ought to be doing the same. Ministers of the gospel are, or ought to be, lifelong students.'[6]

May we not assume that 'the parchments' were 'the holy Scriptures' (3:15), besides their translation into Greek, known as the Septuagint? Lonely, cold and near death, the apostle derived encouragement from God's Word.

We are reminded of William Tyndale, the sixteenth-century Bible translator, who shortly before his death by burning on 6 October 1536 was imprisoned in a cold cell in Vilvoorde, Belgium. He asked for a cloak, a woollen shirt, a warm cap (because of the approaching winter) and, most of all, his Hebrew Bible to be brought to him.

Paul's heartfelt love

Greetings to fellow-workers now in Ephesus (vv. 19–21) and a final benediction (v. 22) bring Paul's second letter to Timothy to a close. Paul wants to express his love for these believers: 'He wants God's people to know that he loves them; and he wants God's people to know that God's people genuinely love them.'[7] Do we show, and express, this kind of love for brothers and sisters in Christ?

One of Paul's companions was Trophimus, whom the apostle left 'sick in Miletus' (v. 20). 'It must have been hard for Trophimus to be left behind at Miletus, only thirty-sixty miles south of his home in Ephesus. And it must have been a sorrowful experience for Paul to discover that he did not at this occasion receive from the Lord the power to heal.'[8]

Christ's presence

Paul's final prayer for Timothy is that he will know Christ's presence and his grace: 'The Lord be with your spirit. Grace be with you' (v. 22). Soon, the man who had treated Timothy like his son would be martyred. Nevertheless, the Lord who stood with Paul would stand with Timothy.

Notes

1 *The MacArthur Study Bible, New King James Version* (Dallas: Word, 1997), p. 1881.

2 **Michael Bentley,** *Passing on the Truth: 1 and 2 Timothy Simply Explained* (Welwyn Commentary; Darlington: Evangelical Press, 1997), p. 298.

3 See 'Appendix 2: Old Testament Appearances of God—Theophanies', in my book *Christ in Exodus* (London: Grace Publications, 2010), pp. 148–150.

4 **John Calvin,** *Commentaries on the Epistles of Paul to Timothy, Titus and Philemon,* tr. Revd William Pringle (Edinburgh: Calvin Translation Society, 1856), p. 271.

5 **William Hendriksen,** *1 & 2 Timothy and Titus* (London: Banner of Truth, 1960), p. 327.

6 **J. Ligon Duncan,** in **Don Carson, (ed.),** *Entrusted with the Gospel: Pastoral Expositions of 2 Timothy* (Nottingham: IVP, 2010), p. 140.

7 Ibid., p. 146.

8 **Hendriksen,** *1 & 2 Timothy and Titus,* p. 332.

The great Shepherd (Heb. 13:20–21, 25)

May the God of peace, who through the blood of the eternal covenant brought back from the dead our Lord Jesus, that great Shepherd of the sheep, equip you with everything good for doing his will, and may he work in us what is pleasing to him, through Jesus Christ, to whom be glory for ever and ever. Amen ... Grace be with you all.

I magine two people at a motorway service station. 'Shall we drive on or go back home?' they ask each other. The weather is appalling: heavy rain, thunder and lightning are making visibility difficult. To reach their destination, they must drive on. But would it be easier to go home? Like these two travellers, the Hebrews were asking themselves, 'Shall we continue our journey to heaven or shall we go back home to Judaism?' What had prompted this question? A storm of persecution from families and friends. Doubts and fears made visibility difficult; they had taken their eyes off Christ and the wonderful destination of heaven.

The Hebrews were wavering. Hebrews 13:20–21 is the prayer of a mature Christian for wavering believers. The writer commends them to the tender care of the great Shepherd. It is appropriate that he calls Christ 'the great Shepherd' in a letter which majors on the superiority of Christ. If we prayed this prayer for one another, perhaps fewer Christians would waver.

The God of peace
Verse 20 focuses on what God has done for us in Christ. He brought him

back from the dead—evidence that he accepted Christ's atoning sacrifice for us and that we are therefore justified (Rom. 4:25).

Verse 21 is about what God is doing in us—he 'equips' us for holy living and useful service. We may say that verse 20 is about salvation (how we became Christians) and verse 21 is about sanctification (how we ought to live as Christians).

The writer addresses his prayer to 'the God of peace' because these Hebrews were like sailors in a hurricane. The storms of temptations and trials were howling around them, but God is able to give perfect peace to those who trust him. He gives tranquillity in the tempest (Isa. 26:3; Phil. 4:6–9).

Moreover, this title reminds us that by nature we are enemies of God—but Christ, 'the Prince of Peace', reconciles us to God (Ps. 51:5, 10; Rom. 5:10; 8:6–8; Col. 1:21–22).

The Shepherd's death

The writer highlights the Shepherd's death in the words 'through the blood of the eternal covenant' (v. 20). 'Blood' indicates a life violently taken by wicked men—a *painful* death. Every muscle of Christ's body screamed with pain as he hung for hours on the cross.

The word 'blood' also speaks of *propitiation*. Sin deserves death—that of either the sinner or a substitute. In the Old Testament, the priests killed sacrificial animals, but their blood could never 'take away sins' (Heb. 10:4). However, Christ, the Lamb of God, died once for all, in the place of the lambs. He bore his people's sin and took the wrath of God upon himself. The Shepherd became the Lamb led to the slaughter (Isa. 53:6–7).

The Shepherd's death was also *particular*—he did not die for all mankind but only for his sheep. This doctrine, known as 'particular redemption', is wrapped up in the word 'covenant'. To quote the Puritan pastor and Bible scholar John Owen, 'He is the only Shepherd; and he is the

Shepherd only of his sheep … He did not lay down his life for the whole of mankind, but for the flock given and committed unto him by his father.'[1]

The 'eternal covenant' means that, before time began, God the Father gave the sheep to his Son, who undertook to visit earth and die for them. It also indicates that the Son has promised to receive each one of his sheep when they return to him in repentance and faith. He has pledged to bring each one of his sheep to heaven; none of the sheep will lose its way on the path to everlasting life.

If Christ had died for everyone, there would be some in hell for whom he had died. Did Christ die for some people in vain? No; Jesus clearly taught the doctrines of election and particular redemption in the Gospel of John (6:37–40; 10:11, 27–30; 17:6, 9, 20–21, 24).

The Shepherd's resurrection

Verse 20 mentions 'the God of peace, who … brought back from the dead our Lord Jesus'. God raised Christ from the grave and welcomed him back into heaven to show his satisfaction with the atoning work of his Son on the cross. We may therefore go boldly to 'the God of peace' and ask for pardon for our sins. God will not turn away any penitent sinner who approaches him through Christ.

Besides this, we as Christ's sheep know that one day God will raise us from our graves and give us bodies—or change us instantly if we are alive at Christ's return. The power that raised Christ from the dead also works in us (1 Cor. 15:51–57; Eph. 1:18–21; 1 Thes. 4:13–18).

The work of God

What of the second part of the benediction in verse 21? The word 'equip' is a translation of the Greek word *katartidzo*, which can mean 'to set a broken bone', 'to mend a broken net' or 'to equip an army for battle'. To pray that God will equip Christians is to pray for strength, for usefulness and for courage in spiritual warfare.

By tracing this word *katartidzo* in the New Testament, we can discover the tools that God uses to equip his people to become mature and useful Christians.

- The Word of God (2 Tim. 3:16–17)
- Prayer (1 Thes. 3:10—translated as 'supply')
- Spiritual leaders (Eph. 4:11–12—translated as 'prepare')
- Fellow-believers (Gal. 6:1—translated as 'restore')
- Suffering (1 Peter 5:10—translated as 'restore')

The will of God

Phil Arthur explains the results of this equipping: 'They were not merely to do the will of God in a partial and limited way, but to bring the whole of their lives into conformity with it.'[2] It is as we do God's will that our lives please him.

The writer to the Hebrews highlights God's sovereign work and our human activity. God works in us; we do his will. As Paul declared, '… it is God who works in you to will and to act according to his good purpose' (Phil. 2:13).

What is God's will? It is that we should do 'everything good' (v. 21)—not to *become* Christians but because we *are* Christians. Like fruit that shows that a tree is alive, so good works prove that believers have spiritual life.

Believers often have difficulty discerning God's will when facing major decisions. Here is a bite-sized piece of advice that is often given: the will of God can never lead you where the grace of God cannot keep you.

Before entering into a questionable activity, ask yourself, 'Can I pray about this? What if Christ should return and find me doing this?' Before entering into a friendship, especially one that could lead to marriage, ask yourself, 'Can we pray and read God's Word together?' We should always desire to do 'what is pleasing to him' (v. 21).

The worship of God

This benediction ends with the words 'through Jesus Christ, to whom be glory for ever and ever. Amen'. We worship God 'through Jesus Christ', the great Shepherd who died for us. His blood paves the way to God; it gives us confidence to approach God's throne (10:19–20).

Commentators debate whether the writer to the Hebrews is here ascribing the glory to God or to Christ. Surely we should give glory to both, because both are God. John Owen says, 'All grace is from God, and through Christ, and so this ascription of glory may be taken as jointly to the Father and to the Son.'[3]

Is worship for Sundays only, and something that we only do in a religious building? No! Living our lives for God, wherever we are and whatever company we are in, is a 'spiritual act of worship' (Rom. 12:1). Writing to the Corinthians, Paul said, 'So whether you eat or drink or whatever you do, do it all for the glory of God' (1 Cor. 10:31). Make the benediction in Hebrews 13:20–21 your prayer for the believers in your church!

God's grace

Hebrews ends with a brief benediction: 'Grace be with you all' (v. 25). Grace is 'the sunshine of God's love, the gentle rain of mercy' by which 'impoverished sinners are endowed with eternal wealth—the unsearchable riches of Christ', explains Edgar Andrews.[4] For the word 'all', he imagines the writer putting 'his arms around them *all* in one final protective gesture of affection. It is a perfect note on which to end.'[5]

Notes

1 **John Owen,** *Hebrews: The Epistle of Warning* (Grand Rapids, MI: Kregel, 1953), p. 281.

2 **J. Philip Arthur,** *No Turning Back: An Exposition of the Epistle to the Hebrews* (London: Grace Publications, 2002), p. 233.

Chapter 20

3 **Owen,** *Hebrews*, p. 282.

4 **Edgar Andrews,** *A Glorious High Throne: Hebrews Simply Explained* (Welwyn Commentary; Darlington: Evangelical Press, 2003), p. 526.

5 Ibid.

Eternal glory
(1 Peter 5:10–11, 14)

And the God of all grace, who called you to his eternal glory in Christ, after you have suffered a little while, will himself restore you and make you strong, firm and steadfast. To him be the power for ever and ever. Amen ... Peace to all of you who are in Christ.

The NIV gives a statement of fact: 'And the God of all grace ... will himself restore you.' On the other hand, the NKJV is in the form of a prayer: 'But may the God of all grace ... settle you.' I think that we should combine both ideas and see Peter's words as a benediction-prayer for first-century suffering Christians and, therefore, a model of how we ought to pray for distressed fellow-believers.

It is important not to overlook the link-word 'And', because the preceding verses indicate reasons for the apostle's supplication. Prayer is the remedy for pride and promotes 'humility towards one another' (vv. 5–6). Prayer is also essential for casting our care on the Lord (v. 7). By prayer we resist the devil, who 'prowls around like a roaring lion looking for someone to devour' (v. 8). Prayer creates a sympathetic bond with fellow-sufferers (v. 9).

Eternal glory

The apostle Peter directs his readers' thoughts to 'eternal glory' before he reminds them of their present suffering. Present suffering paves the way to future glory. We gain persevering grace as we 'fix our eyes on Jesus, the author and perfecter of our faith, who for the joy set before him endured the cross, scorning its shame, and sat down at the right hand of the throne of God' (Heb. 12:2).

God will welcome us into 'eternal glory' because Christ has given us eternal life. Jesus said, 'My sheep listen to my voice; I know them, and they follow me. I give them eternal life, and they shall never perish; no one can snatch them out of my hand. My Father, who has given them to me, is greater than all; no one can snatch them out of my Father's hand' (John 10:27–29). If one of Christ's sheep could be lost, then 'Jesus must have meant "lend" when he said "give", and "temporary" when he said "eternal" and "perhaps" when he said "never"'.[1]

What is the significance of 'glory' (v. 10)? Heaven will be glorious—more glorious than we can ever imagine. When we reach heaven, we will respond as the Queen of Sheba did when she saw Solomon's wealth and heard his wisdom: 'not even half was told me' (1 Kings 10:7). We will see the glorious God: Father, Son and Holy Spirit. We will also witness the answer to Jesus's prayer: 'Father, I want those you have given me to be with me where I am, and to see my glory, the glory you have given me because you loved me before the creation of the world' (John 17:24). At that time he 'will transform our lowly bodies so that they will be like his glorious body' (Phil. 3:21). Then we will receive 'the crown of righteousness' from 'the Lord, the righteous Judge' (2 Tim. 4:8). God rewards us for what he has accomplished in and through us!

The apostle Peter tells us in 1 Peter 5 that we will enter 'eternal glory' because of God's grace ('the God of all grace'), God's call ('who called you') and God's Son ('in Christ'). Grace is the spontaneous overflowing of God's love in the gift of salvation to those who deserve nothing but punishment for their sins. Grace is a motif running through Peter's first letter (1:2, 10, 13; 4:10; 5:5, 10, 12). 'God of all grace' assures us that God's grace is sufficient in every situation.

God's grace becomes our experience through God's call. His call is more than an invitation; it is a divine summons which we must obey to obtain 'eternal glory'. Christ, by his death, opened the door to 'eternal glory'. He died so that we will live for ever.

Temporal suffering

You can only enter 'eternal glory ... after you have suffered a little while'; the implication is that suffering is a normal part of the Christian life. In the previous verse, Peter mentions 'your brothers throughout the world [who] are undergoing the same kind of sufferings' (v. 9). Paul's warning to young Timothy also highlights this fact: 'In fact, everyone who wants to live a godly life in Christ Jesus will be persecuted' (2 Tim. 3:12). For some believers, persecution takes the form of imprisonment, torture and even death; for others, persecution comes as ridicule, apathy or misunderstanding from family because of their convictions (1 Peter 4:4). The term 'suffered' at 5:10 is broader than persecution; it includes 'grief in all kinds of trials' (1:6) and 'anxiety' (5:7). Some of our cares arise because of the activity of Satan, who behaves like a hungry, roaring lion (5:8).

Our suffering, for whatever reason and from whatever source (human or demonic), does not last for ever; it is only for 'a little while'. Back in chapter 1, in the context of anticipating our inheritance, Peter wrote, 'In this you greatly rejoice, though now for a little while you may have had to suffer grief' (v. 6). A 'little' grief leads to 'eternal glory'! Paul's words to the Corinthians are similar to Peter's: 'For our light and momentary troubles are achieving for us an eternal glory that far outweighs them all. So we fix our eyes not on what is seen, but on what is unseen. For what is seen is temporary, but what is unseen is eternal' (2 Cor. 4:17–18).

Paul described his 'light and momentary troubles' in verses 8–12 of that chapter and in 2 Corinthians 11:23–29. He suffered more than most men! In what sense were these sufferings 'light'? Hodge's comments are helpful:

The Bible does not teach, either by precept or example, that Christians are to bear pain as though it were not pain or bereavements as though they caused no sorrow … It was only by bringing these sufferings into comparison with eternal glory that they dwindled into insignificance. So also when the apostle says that his afflictions were for a moment, it is only when compared with eternity. They were not momentary so far as the present life was concerned. They lasted from his conversion to his martyrdom. His Christian life was a protracted dying. But what is the longest life compared to everlasting ages? … Afflictions are the cause of eternal glory. Not the meritorious cause, but still the procuring cause. God has seen fit to reveal his purpose not only to reward with exceeding joy the afflictions of his people, but to make those afflictions the means of working out that joy.[2]

The Christian knows that the light of eternal glory shines at the end of the dark tunnel of suffering.

In the opening chapter of Peter's first letter, he explains God's purpose in suffering: 'These ['all kinds of trials', v. 6] have come so that your faith—of greater worth than gold, which perishes even though refined by fire—may be proved genuine' (v. 7). Like gold, our faith is put in the fire of trials to see if it is real and to get rid of blemishes. Malachi, the Jewish prophet, also used this metaphor of precious metal in the fire: 'He [God] will sit as a refiner and purifier of silver; he will purify the Levites and refine them like gold and silver' (Mal. 3:3). The refiner sits because he is carefully watching the silver so that it does not overheat. The divine Refiner sits until he sees his own likeness in the tried believer. Refining leads to greater love for Christ and even to 'an inexpressible and glorious joy' (1 Peter 1:8). Why should we love Christ when he tests us? Because it is then that we feel his unsurpassed sympathy (Heb. 4:15–16).

What God will do

Until we enjoy 'eternal glory', 'the God of all grace … will himself restore you and make you strong, firm and steadfast'.

The Greek word translated 'restore' means 'to mend that which is broken'; it is used in Mark 1:19, where we read that James and John were 'mending their nets' (NKJV). They were mending their nets to make them useful for more fishing. God mends our lives that are broken by sin and battered by suffering in the storms of life. He saves us and equips us to serve him. He restores broken hearts and shows the beauty of grace in our lives.

The Greek word behind 'strong' ('strengthen', NKJV) was used by Christ when he spoke to Peter shortly before he denied his Master: 'Simon, Simon, Satan has asked to sift you as wheat. But I have prayed for you, Simon, that your faith may not fail. And when you have turned back, *strengthen* your brothers' (Luke 22:31–32, emphasis added). Peter fulfilled his gracious Saviour's command through his preaching and by writing two letters to encourage persecuted Christians.

The Greek behind 'firm and steadfast' means 'to lay a foundation'. Was Peter thinking of Jesus's parable of the two builders? One man built his house on rock, a solid foundation; therefore it stood in the storms. Another man built his house on sand; it 'fell with a great crash' when 'the winds blew and beat' against it (Matt. 7:24–27). Lives built on Christ and his Word stand firm in trials and temptations (1 Cor. 3:9–15).

We ought to notice the word 'himself'—'God … will himself restore you'—which indicates God's personal love for, and care of, each one of his children.

Power and glory

In verse 11 the word 'power' signifies that God is the divine Ruler who controls the entire universe. He is more powerful than human kings or emperors. He is the Monarch who cannot be removed from his throne by enemies or by death. He is mightier than the devil (v. 8) and demonic powers (Eph. 6:12). Peter declares that God reigns 'for ever and ever' and adds 'Amen', which is both an affirmation that what God decrees will happen and a prayer for God's will to be done (v. 10).

Peter combines power with glory in the brief doxology in the previous chapter: 'To him be the glory and the power for ever and ever. Amen' (4:11). These words are reminiscent of David's prayer in 1 Chronicles 29:10–11:

Praise be to you, O LORD,

God of our father Israel,

from everlasting to everlasting.

Yours, O LORD, is the greatness and the power

and the glory and the majesty and the splendour,

for everything in heaven and earth is yours.

Yours, O LORD, is the kingdom;

you are exalted as head over all.[3]

This ascription of praise anticipates the worship of the redeemed in heaven: 'To him who sits on the throne and to the Lamb be praise and honour and glory and power for ever and ever!' (Rev. 5:13).

Peter's briefer doxology is linked with his encouragement to Christians to use their gifts to serve God's people:

Each one should use whatever gift he has received to serve others, faithfully administering God's grace in its various forms. If anyone speaks, he should do it as one speaking the very words of God. If anyone serves, he should do it with the strength God provides, so that in all things God may be praised through Jesus Christ. To him be the glory and the power for ever and ever. Amen. (4:10–11)

The literal meaning of 'faithfully administering' is 'as good stewards' and 'refers to a manager who is in charge of his master's possessions'.[4] We are answerable to God for the use of his gifts. Does our service prompt fellow-believers to praise God?

Peace

The apostle Peter concludes his first letter with a prayer: 'Peace to all of you who are in Christ' (v. 14). In Christ, we have peace with God and with one another.

Notes

1 **Terence Peter Crosby,** meditation for 4 December, in *365 Days with Spurgeon*, vol. i (Epsom: Day One, 1998).

2 **Charles Hodge,** *Commentary on the Second Epistle to the Corinthians* (Geneva Commentary; Edinburgh: Banner of Truth, 1959; electronic edn., STEP Files © QuickVerse).

3 Compare 1 Chronicles 29:10–11 with the ending of the Lord's Prayer in Matthew 6:13 (NKJV). For an excellent exposition of this prayer read **Derek Prime,** *The Lord's Prayer for Today* (Leominster: Day One, 2004).

4 **Simon J. Kistemaker,** *Peter and Jude* (New Testament Commentary; Welwyn: Evangelical Press, 1987), p. 169.

Growing in grace (2 Peter 3:18)

But grow in the grace and knowledge of our Lord and Saviour Jesus Christ. To him be glory both now and for ever! Amen.

My worried mother took me to the doctor and said, 'Why isn't he growing?' 'Don't worry,' he told her, 'some children are small for their age.' I eventually grew up to marry Maureen, who is shorter than me!

At a certain age we stop growing physically, but we should always be growing spiritually. This is the reason why the apostle Peter concludes his second letter with a prayer for the spiritual growth of his readers. The apostle's doxology echoes his opening greeting (1:2) and also picks up the theme of growing in grace from the first chapter (1:5–9).

Evidence of birth

We learn from Peter's first letter that spiritual growth is evidence of the 'new birth' (1 Peter 1:3; 2:2). But why do we receive a new birth from God? It is because he has chosen us (1:2). Those whom God has chosen are 'all the more eager to make [their] calling and election sure' (2 Peter 1:10). We do this as we 'grow in the grace and knowledge of our Lord and Saviour Jesus Christ' (3:18).

Just as a child grows gradually from infancy, through childhood and teenage years, into an adult, so we are to grow from newborn believers into mature Christians. Physically and spiritually, some grow more quickly than others, but no growth at all indicates that there is no life or a serious problem.

Signs of growth

The word 'But' links verse 18 to the context, where we find indications of how to grow. The growing Christian develops discernment, so that he or she is not 'carried away by the error of lawless men' (v. 17). Paul makes a similar point in his letter to the Ephesians, where he says that mature believers 'will no longer be infants, tossed back and forth by the waves, and blown here and there by every wind of teaching and by the cunning and craftiness of men in their deceitful scheming. Instead, speaking the truth in love, we will in all things grow up into him who is the Head, that is, Christ' (Eph. 4:14–15).

Peter has reminded his readers of 'the words spoken in the past by the holy prophets and the command given by our Lord and Saviour through your apostles' (3:2). The words of the prophets and apostles are now written in the Bible. Understanding God's Word prevents us from being 'carried away' and from falling from our 'secure position' (v. 17).

Peter is not saying that a genuine Christian can fall away from Christ. Such a thought would contradict the apostle's teaching in 1 Peter 1:4–5, where we read that we have an inheritance 'kept in heaven', and that we ourselves are 'kept by the power of God' (NKJV) to enjoy that everlasting inheritance. To 'fall from your secure position' means that we do not obey God's Word and for this reason we are not growing in grace.

Christians grow from infancy to maturity by feeding on God's Word. In his first letter Peter wrote, 'Like newborn babies, crave pure spiritual milk, so that by it you may grow up in your salvation, now that you have tasted that the Lord is good' (1 Peter 2:2–3).

The writer to the Hebrews complains that his readers are 'slow to learn'. He writes,

In fact, though by this time you ought to be teachers, you need someone to teach you the elementary truths of God's word all over again. You need milk, not solid food! Anyone who lives on milk, being still an infant, is not acquainted with the teaching about righteousness. But solid food is for the mature, who by constant use have trained themselves to distinguish good from evil.   (Heb. 5:11–14)

Likewise, Paul was sad that the Corinthians were 'mere infants in Christ' to whom he gave 'milk, not solid food'; even as he was writing, they were 'still not ready' for it. Divisions within the church and factions supporting favourite preachers were a display of childish behaviour (1 Cor. 3:1–4).

We need 'solid food', but parts of God's Word, especially some of Paul's letters, 'are hard to understand, which ignorant and unstable people distort, as they do the other Scriptures, to their own destruction' (1 Peter 3:16). We ought to notice that Peter places Paul's writings on a par with 'the other Scriptures': the writings which we now know as the Old Testament.

The 'ignorant and unstable people' are the 'scoffers' who refuse to believe that Christ is coming, even though this doctrine was taught by both Paul and Peter (v. 3).

They twist the meaning of Scripture so that the truth of God's revelation is turned into a lie. As torturers make a victim on the rack say the opposite of the truth, so the false teachers place Scripture on the rack and distort its message … Ultimately they face God, who has revealed himself in his Word and who turns Scripture against his adversaries to their own destruction.[1]

Another mark of the growing Christian is that he or she pursues holiness rather than happiness. Holiness is likeness to Christ, who was 'a lamb without blemish or defect' (1 Peter 1:19). The believer makes 'every effort to be found spotless, blameless and at peace with [God]'

(2 Peter 3:14). His or her conduct is the exact opposite of that of the false teachers, who are 'blots and blemishes' (2:13). The terms 'spotless' and 'blameless' do not mean that we are sinless—perfection is impossible while on earth—but indicate sincerity. We sincerely aspire to live godly lives, even though we fail! We aim to match our beliefs with our behaviour.

Biblical examples of people who lived blamelessly are Noah (Gen. 6:9), Joseph (see, for example, Gen. 39), Job (Job 1:8; 2:3), Daniel (Dan. 6:5), Zechariah and his wife, Elizabeth (Luke 1:5–6), Mary, the Saviour's mother (Luke 1:26–30), and aged Simeon and Anna (Luke 2:25–38). Place alongside these models the exhortations of Paul to the Philippians: 'Do everything without complaining or arguing, so that you may become blameless and pure, children of God without fault in a crooked and depraved generation' (Phil. 2:14–15). We have seen in previous chapters that Paul prayed that the Thessalonians would live blamelessly (1 Thes. 3:11–13; 5:23–24).

Christ's second coming is a stimulus to holy living. He comes to destroy this world by fire, but from the ashes will arise 'a new heaven and a new earth, the home of righteousness' (2 Peter 3:13). The believer is 'looking forward to this' with eager anticipation (v. 14). However, the Saviour's return poses a serious question: '… what kind of people ought you to be? You ought to live holy and godly lives as you look forward to the day of God and speed its coming' (vv. 11–12). Believers with their thoughts on Jesus's return will grow in grace.

In what sense can we 'speed' Christ's coming? Some commentators suggest alternative translations, such as the marginal NIV reading: 'as you wait eagerly for the day of God to come'. Nevertheless, Kistemaker argues that 'speed its coming' is the correct rendering.[2] This would then link to Paul's prayer 'Come, O Lord!' (1 Cor. 16:22) and the petition in what we know as the Lord's Prayer: 'your kingdom come, your will be done on earth as it is in heaven' (Matt. 6:10). In some way that we do not yet understand, our holy living and our prayers bring the Lord's coming nearer.

Knowledge of Christ

The established Christian is more interested in 'growing in the grace' than in receiving gifts. The immature Corinthians excelled in gifts (1 Cor. 1:7; 12) but were lacking in the greatest gift of all—love for God and for fellow-saints (1 Cor. 13). Most of all, the believer wants to know the Lord Jesus Christ. This 'knowledge' is more than knowing about Christ; it is knowing him personally and loving him increasingly as year succeeds year.

Almost thirty years after his conversion, Paul, a gifted apostle and writer of Scripture, wrote that he longed to know Christ better:

But whatever was to my profit I now consider loss for the sake of Christ. What is more, I consider everything a loss compared to the surpassing greatness of knowing Christ Jesus my Lord, for whose sake I have lost all things. I consider them rubbish, that I may gain Christ and be found in him, not having a righteousness of my own that comes from the law, but that which is through faith in Christ—the righteousness that comes from God and is by faith. I want to know Christ and the power of his resurrection and the fellowship of sharing in his sufferings, becoming like him in his death, and so, somehow, to attain to the resurrection from the dead.   (Phil. 3:7–11)

The Christian who wants to grow in grace desires the glory of Christ: 'To him be glory both now and for ever!' (2 Peter 3:18). Like John the Baptist, the growing Christian wants Christ to become greater and him- or herself to become less (John 3:30). By addressing this doxology to Christ rather than to God, the apostle is affirming that Jesus is God and worthy of our praise now and for ever.

What better word could Peter use to conclude his letter than 'Amen', which means 'so be it'?

Notes

1 **Simon J. Kistemaker,** *Peter and Jude* (New Testament Commentary; Welwyn: Evangelical Press, 1987), p. 346.
2 Ibid., p. 338.

God is able
(Jude 24–25)

To him who is able to keep you from falling and to present you before his glorious presence without fault and with great joy—to the only God our Saviour be glory, majesty, power and authority, through Jesus Christ our Lord, before all ages, now and for evermore! Amen.

Jude, also known as Judas, half-brother of Jesus (Matt. 13:55), wrote this letter (v. 1) to Christians struggling with false teachers (v. 4). He wanted to write about salvation, but the threat of false teachers made it necessary to deal with this urgent issue (v. 3). We may compare Jude's short letter to a piece of music, which is sometimes deep and sad but whose closing finale is exquisite. Three themes emerge from this benediction: protection, presentation and praise.

Protection

Jude begins and ends his letter by focusing on God's keeping power. We read in verse 1 that believers are 'kept by Jesus Christ', and in verse 24 that God 'is able to keep you from falling'. Surrounded by cunning false teachers, we can depend on God's keeping power. He will never fail us. To say that God 'is able' is to proclaim that he is sovereign and powerful; therefore, not one believer will lose his or her salvation.

It is clear from Jude's letter that God's power does not negate our responsibility. We are to keep ourselves 'in God's love' (v. 21). This means that we remain 'within the circle of God's love'.[1] True children of God can never stray beyond their Father's love; however, they may, through sin, lose the comfort of that love and the joy of salvation. Penitent David prayed,

Create in me a pure heart, O God,
    and renew a steadfast spirit within me.
Do not cast me from your presence
    or take your Holy Spirit from me.
Restore to me the joy of your salvation
    and grant me a willing spirit, to sustain me.
Then I will teach transgressors your ways,
    and sinners will turn back to you. (Ps. 51:10–13)

We keep ourselves 'in God's love' by frequently reflecting on Scriptures that declare his unchanging love for us; for example, Isaiah 49:15–16; Jeremiah 31:3; Romans 8:28–39; and 1 John 4:9–10.

The apostle Peter also links God's power and human responsibility when he states that Christians 'through faith are shielded by God's power' (1 Peter 1:5). Disobedient believers might, for a while, go back to their old sinful ways, but they can never become reprobates. The prodigals return with broken hearts to the warm embrace of the waiting Father (Luke 15:11–24). The word 'shielded' contains the idea of God protecting his people from danger. God, who protected Noah from the raging waters of the Flood, keeps us safe in the storms of temptations, trials and false teaching. The ark of the church will never sink.

The word translated 'falling' which Jude uses in verse 24 comes from the world of horse riding: 'God is able to keep you from falling as if you were a horse rider … He is holding the reins of your life and he is able to guide you and keep you from falling and to put you on the right track and bring you safely home.'[2] We may fall over on the journey to heaven, but we can never fall away from Christ. The genuine Christian will never stumble into hell.

Presentation

God will 'present you before his glorious presence without fault and with great joy'. The word 'present' looks back to the Old Testament animal sacrifices presented by Jewish priests on behalf of sinners; these sacrifices that could never 'take away sins' (Heb. 10:11) pointed forward to Christ, the sinless Lamb of God. God's wrath fell on him when he bore our sins: 'Christ died for sins once for all, the righteous for the unrighteous, to bring you to God' (1 Peter 3:18). It is because of Christ's sinless life and his atoning death that God will present us 'without fault' in heaven. Then we shall be like Christ, in fulfilment of God's eternal purpose that we should be 'conformed to the likeness of his Son' (Rom. 8:29).

Now we often lament with Paul, 'What a wretched man I am! Who will rescue me from this body of death?' (Rom. 7:24). *Then* we will have a glorious body and a soul that is free from indwelling sin (Phil. 3:21). Meanwhile, we present ourselves as 'living sacrifices' to God—this is our 'spiritual act of worship' (Rom. 12:1). Godly daily living is an essential part of worshipping God.

Is the 'great joy' in Jude's benediction the joy of believers or the joy of Christ? I suggest that it includes both. 'Christians are not filled with terror but with joy when they enter the presence of God.'[3] Christ will also know joy when all the elect, for whom he died, are gathered safely into heaven. Anticipating this moment, Christ prayed, 'I protected them and kept them safe ... None has been lost' (John 17:12). In that same prayer, Christ desired that those given to him by the Father would 'see my glory, the glory you have given me because you loved me before the creation of the world' (17:24). The fulfilment of this prayer will give the Lord 'great joy'!

Jude's words are similar to those of Paul in Ephesians 5:27, where we read that Christ died to wash his bride, the church, 'to present her to himself as a radiant church, without stain or wrinkle or any other blemish, but holy and blameless'. Commentating on this verse

Hendriksen writes, 'She owes all her beauty to him, the bridegroom.' He adds, 'Is not this marvellous welcome which the bride will receive also *her* supreme honour? Does it not indicate that she is and will forever remain the object of everlasting delight?'4 Hendriksen quotes Zephaniah 3:17: 'The LORD your God is with you, he is mighty to save. He will take great delight in you, he will quiet you with his love, he will rejoice over you with singing.' The radiant bride in heaven will not admire her wedding dress but will gaze into the face of her beloved bridegroom!

Praise

Jude ends his delightful benediction with praise to God: 'to the only God our Saviour be glory, majesty, power and authority, through Jesus Christ our Lord, before all ages, now and for evermore! Amen.' There are variations in the translations. The NIV emphasizes the uniqueness of God, reading 'to the only God our Saviour', a description rooted in passages such as Deuteronomy 6:4—'Hear, O Israel: The LORD our God, the LORD is one'—and Exodus 15:2—'The LORD is my strength and my song; he has become my salvation. He is my God, and I will praise him, my father's God, and I will exalt him.' God alone is the Saviour of his people.

The KJV highlights God's wisdom—'To the only wise God our Saviour'—and recalls passages such as 1 Timothy 1:17 ('Now to the King eternal, immortal, invisible, the only God, be honour and glory for ever and ever. Amen') and Isaiah 40:12–14:

Who has measured the waters in the hollow of his hand,
or with the breadth of his hand marked off the heavens?
Who has held the dust of the earth in a basket,
or weighed the mountains on the scales
and the hills in a balance?
Who has understood the mind of the LORD,
or instructed him as his counsellor?

Chapter 23

Whom did the LORD consult to enlighten him,
and who taught him the right way?
Who was it that taught him knowledge
or showed him the path of understanding?

Compare these texts with Romans 16:27—'to the only wise God'—and 1 Timothy 6:15–16—'God … who alone is immortal' (we considered these two texts in Chs. 7 and 18). Salvation displays the wisdom of God.

Four divine attributes

Jude focuses on four divine attributes for which we ought to praise God.

GLORY

This is the radiance or splendour of God, as seen by Moses (Exod. 33:12–21), Isaiah (Isa. 6:1–13) and three of Jesus's disciples, Peter, James and John, at his Transfiguration (Matt. 17:1–12). We see his glory in Christ (2 Cor. 4:6). We reveal God's glory by our good deeds (Matt. 5:16). We will reflect God's glory in heaven (Rom. 8:18).

MAJESTY

The Greek word for this is found only here and in Hebrews 1:3, where we read that Christ 'sat down at the right hand of the Majesty in heaven', and in Hebrews 8:1, where we read that Christ our High Priest 'sat down at the right hand of the throne of the Majesty in heaven'. God is the King who works for the good of his people (Rom. 8:28).

POWER AND AUTHORITY

Both words emphasize the supremacy of God who is the sovereign Ruler of the entire universe.

Jesus came to earth to reveal God's glory, majesty, power and authority; therefore, Jude adds the phrase 'through Jesus Christ our

Lord'. The words 'before all ages, now and for evermore' cover past, present and future; God is the eternal and unchanging King whom the saints will adore ceaselessly for eternity. 'Amen'—'so be it'—is a fitting conclusion to this sublime doxology.

If you desire God's 'glory', worship him, because he is God. If you proclaim his 'majesty, power and authority', obey him, because he is King.

Notes

1 **Simon J. Kistemaker,** *Peter and Jude* (New Testament Commentary; Welwyn: Evangelical Press, 1987), p. 406.

2 **John Benton,** *Slandering Angels: The Message of Jude* (Welwyn Commentary; Darlington: Evangelical Press, 1999), pp. 165–166. See also **Kistemaker,** *Peter and Jude*, p. 411.

3 **Kistemaker,** *Peter and Jude*, p. 411.

4 **William Hendriksen,** *Ephesians* (New Testament Commentary; London: Banner of Truth, 1967), pp. 553–554.

Loved and freed (Rev. 1:4–7)

John, To the seven churches in the province of Asia: Grace and peace to you from him who is, and who was, and who is to come, and from the seven spirits before his throne, and from Jesus Christ, who is the faithful witness, the firstborn from the dead, and the ruler of the kings of the earth. To him who loves us and has freed us from our sins by his blood, and has made us to be a kingdom and priests to serve his God and Father—to him be glory and power for ever and ever! Amen.

Look, he is coming with the clouds,
    and every eye will see him,
even those who pierced him;
    and all the peoples of the earth will mourn because of him.
So shall it be! Amen.

There are three reasons why every Christian should study the book of Revelation. Firstly, it is a gift from God: 'The revelation ... which God gave' (1:1). This book is an essential part of God's inerrant Word. Secondly, it is about Christ: 'The revelation of Jesus Christ' (v. 1). Thirdly, it is good for our souls: 'Blessed is the one who reads the words of this prophecy, and blessed are those who hear it and take to heart what is written in it, because the time is near' (v. 3). What blessing comes through reading Revelation? A greater devotion to Christ and a desire to see his glory!

The Greek behind the title 'Revelation' means 'unveiling'. The focal point of this revelation is the Lord Jesus Christ. Richard Brooks has listed some of the numerous titles of Christ found in Revelation.[1] Several of these designations occur in benedictions and doxologies; for example, in the verses quoted above, Christ is 'the faithful witness, the firstborn from the dead, and the ruler of the kings of the earth (v. 5).

Guidelines for interpretation[2]

Revelation is a book of symbolism, as indicated by the words 'made it known' (v. 1; the literal Greek is 'signified'). We must therefore be cautious in our interpretation of the visions and symbols that are often rooted in the Old Testament.[3] For example, Revelation 1:7 alludes to Zechariah 12:10–14, and verses 12–13 look back to the lampstand in the tabernacle (Exod. 25:31–40; 37:17–24) and also refer to Zechariah 4:2. The description of Christ in verse 13 is similar to that of the Ancient of Days in Daniel 7:9–10. Whenever we read the Bible, whether Old or New Testament, we should compare Scripture with Scripture.

We should also remember that God gave this revelation of Christ to encourage persecuted believers. The aged apostle John was exiled by the Roman emperor Domitian (reigned AD 81–96) to Patmos, an island in the Aegean Sea between Greece and Turkey (v. 9). God directed John's eyes away from his suffering to the glorious Saviour who is the Lamb enthroned in heaven (5:1–14). God gave to the author of the fourth Gospel and three short letters the command to write 'everything he saw' (1:2) for the benefit of the seven churches in Asia Minor, now part of Turkey (1:4, 11; chs. 2–3).

John received this 'revelation of Jesus Christ' on 'the Lord's Day', when he 'was in the Spirit' (1:10). 'He sees, indeed, but not with physical eyes. He hears, but not with physical ears. He is in direct spiritual contact with his Saviour.'[4]

The words 'what must soon take place' (v. 1) show that the message of Revelation had immediate relevance to first-century believers; however, this message is for Christians in every age. We too need to remember that the events of history will reach their climax in the coming of the Lord Jesus Christ.

We have noticed a Trinitarian focus in several benedictions; it is also present in John's (vv. 4–5). I suggest that John's use of the phrase 'Grace and peace to you' (v. 4) indicates that verses 4–5 are a crucial part of the benediction that runs to verse 7. As we have seen in previous chapters, grace and peace are like two melodies occurring frequently in biblical benedictions. Grace is God's unmerited favour; peace is 'the reflection of the smile of God in the heart of the believer who has been reconciled to God through the Lord Jesus Christ'.[5] Who gives believers grace and peace?

God the Father

John describes God as the One 'who is, and who was, and who is to come' (v. 4; 4:8). This description parallels God's words to Moses at the burning bush: 'I AM WHO I AM' (Exod. 3:14). He is eternally present and therefore unchanging; he has no beginning and no end. He is self-existent and therefore depends on no one. In verse 8 God[6] himself speaks and says, 'I am the Alpha and the Omega … who is, and who was, and who is to come, the Almighty.' Alpha and Omega are the first and last letters of the Greek alphabet, the original language of the New Testament. These titles appear again at 21:6 and 22:13, where Christ is also called Alpha and Omega because he is God the Son, equal to God the Father.

Alpha and Omega affirm that God is the beginning and end of history; he controls all things. Just as 'the alpha is connected to the omega, the one must inevitably lead to the other',[7] so all that God has decreed must come to fulfilment; nothing or no one can frustrate his plans. He is 'the Almighty' (v. 8), 'not merely supreme in power, more powerful than all other powers combined; but He is all the power'.[8]

God the Son

Jesus ('Saviour') Christ ('anointed') is 'the faithful witness' (v. 5). He is faithful because he perfectly obeyed God his Father: he lived a sinless life (Heb. 7:26). A witness relates what he has seen. Christ came from heaven, not only to speak about God, but also to show us God; he was God in human flesh. In his Gospel, John declares that 'the Word [i.e. Christ] became flesh and dwelt among us, and we beheld His glory, the glory as of the only begotten of the Father [i.e. he is unique because he is the only uncreated Son of God; he is God's eternal Son], full of grace and truth' (John 1:14, NKJV). Later he adds, 'No one has seen God at any time. The only begotten Son, who is in the bosom of the Father, He has declared Him' (v. 18, NKJV; see also 10:30; 14:8–11). God speaks in his Son—the everlasting Word.

Christ is also 'the firstborn from the dead' (v. 5; compare Col. 1:15–18). In a Jewish family the firstborn son was the most important child and therefore given special privileges and responsibilities. He was the heir of his father's property and possessions. Jesus Christ, the eternal Son of God, is God's beloved (the word used in the NKJV in Matt. 3:17; 17:5).

God gave his precious Son to die a cruel, painful death on a Roman cross so that we might become the adopted sons of God. He is 'the firstborn among many brothers' (Rom. 8:29). Believers are 'God's children' and 'co-heirs with Christ'; they 'share in his sufferings in order that [they] may also share in his glory' (Rom. 8:16–17).

As the 'firstborn from the dead', Christ was the first to receive a resurrection body that was immortal. Christ raised from the dead Jairus's daughter (Mark 5:21–43), a widow's son (Luke 7:11–17) and Lazarus (John 11:1–44), but these all died again later. Jesus said to exiled John, 'Do not be afraid. I am the First and the Last. I am the Living One; I was dead, and behold I am alive for ever and ever! And I hold the keys of death and Hades' (Rev. 1:17–18). It is because of his death and resurrection that our perishable bodies will be changed into imperishable bodies in which we will live for ever (1 Cor. 15:51–57)! Hades 'always refers to death as the condition in which body and soul are separated'.[9]

Christ is 'the ruler of the kings of the earth' (v. 5; 17:14; 19:16; 1 Tim. 1:17). Earthly rulers—even the Roman emperor Domitian—receive their authority from God; all are accountable to him (Rom. 13:1–7). We are to pray 'for kings and all those in authority, that we may live peaceful and quiet lives in all godliness and holiness' (1 Tim. 2:1–2). When Christ comes, everyone, including the mightiest human rulers, will bow before him and 'confess that Jesus Christ is Lord' (Phil. 2:9–11). Better to bow in repentance now, than bow in regretful submission later.

God the Holy Spirit

God's grace and peace flow not only from the Father and from Jesus Christ, but also from 'the seven spirits before his throne' (v. 4). As this clause is sandwiched between John's description of God and of Christ, it can only refer to the Holy Spirit.

Why is the Spirit placed before Christ? The commentators suggest that the answer lies in the plan of the tabernacle. The Jewish tabernacle was a copy of what is in heaven (Heb. 8:5). In the tabernacle, 'the ark in the Holy of Holies represented the throne of God, the lampstand with the seven branches in front of the ark represented the Spirit, while the altar, whose priests and sacrifices pointed to the Lord Jesus Christ, was in the courtyard in front of the Holy Place'.[10]

The Spirit is 'before his [God's] throne' (v. 4). In chapter 4, John sees God the Creator on a throne (4:2, 9–11) and in chapter 5 his attention is drawn to 'a Lamb ... standing in the centre of the throne' (5:6). There is another reference linking the throne and 'the seven spirits' at 4:5. The throne is shared by God the Father, God the Son and God the Holy Spirit.

What is the meaning of 'the seven spirits'? The number seven occurs over forty times in Revelation. Besides seven spirits (1:4; 3:1; 4:5) there are seven churches (1:4), seven golden lampstands (1:12; 2:1), seven stars (1:16; 2:1; 3:1), seven seals (5:1), seven horns and seven eyes (5:6), seven angels with seven trumpets (8:2), seven thunders (10:3), seven heads of the dragon wearing seven diadems (12:3), seven heads of the beast (13:1), seven golden bowls (15:7) and seven kings (17:10). In the Jewish mind, seven was a number of completeness and perfection because God created the world in six days and rested on the seventh day. At the end of the creation week, 'God saw all that he had made, and it was very good' (Gen. 1:31).

We may say, then, that 'the seven spirits' points to the perfection and variety of the Holy Spirit's work in convicting unbelievers of sin and in sustaining the spiritual life of believers (John 14:15–21; 15:26–27; 16:5–16). The persecuted Christians could depend on the powerful presence of God the Holy Spirit to give them comfort and strength—and so can we!

There is an interesting mention of 'the seven spirits' in the letter to the church in Sardis in Revelation 3:1: 'These are the words of him who holds the seven spirits of God and the seven stars.' It was through the Holy Spirit that the spiritually dead stars—the leaders—and the spiritually dead church in Sardis would come to life again! In what sense does Christ hold the Holy Spirit in his hand? He sent the Holy Spirit to his church (John 15:26). Christ gives or withholds his blessing in conversions and spiritual growth according to his sovereign will.

What Christ has done

Verse 5a highlights who Christ is; verses 5b–6 turn the spotlight on what he has done. Verse 7 looks forward to what he will do.

HE LOVED US

Commentators debate the correct tense of this phrase in verse 5: should it read 'loved', as in the NKJV, or 'loves' as in the NIV? 'If he loved us on the cross, will he not love us forever? And if he loves us now, is it not because he loved us on the accursed tree?'[11]

HE HAS FREED US

Should verse 5 read 'washed' (NKJV) or 'freed' (NIV)? Whichever reading we adopt, the meaning is the same: Christ not only died for us, he also applies his atoning power to us.

If we follow the NKVJ rendering, 'washed', the emphasis is on the fact that sin pollutes the soul. Jesus said, 'What comes out of a man is what makes him "unclean". For from within, out of men's hearts, come evil thoughts, sexual immorality, theft, murder, adultery, greed, malice, deceit, lewdness, envy, slander, arrogance and folly. All these evils come from inside and make a man "unclean"' (Mark 7:20–23). He spoke these words to the Pharisees who complained that Christ's disciples had eaten with 'unwashed' hands. Ceremonial washing was a big issue for the self-righteous Pharisees (7:1–5). On another occasion Jesus said to these men, 'You clean the outside of the cup and dish, but inside they are full of greed and self-indulgence. Blind Pharisee! First clean the inside of the cup and dish, and then the outside also will be clean' (Matt. 23:25–26). Neither religious ritual, however elaborate, nor good deeds, however conscientiously performed, can ever wash away sin. In the benediction we praise God, 'who loved us and washed us from our sins in His own blood' (Rev. 1:5, NKJV). Only Christ's blood washes away sin (1 John 1:9).

If we follow the NIV translation, 'freed', the point is that sin enslaves the soul. This spiritual bondage is clearly stated by the apostle Paul in his letter to the Romans: '... the sinful mind is hostile to God. It does not submit to God's law, nor can it do so. Those controlled by the sinful nature cannot please God' (Rom. 8:7–8; see also 6:15–23). Writing to Timothy, Paul states that sinners are in 'the trap of the devil, who has taken them captive to do his will' (2 Tim. 2:26).

Paul's teaching has its roots in Christ's own statements: '... everyone who sins is a slave to sin' (John 8:34). Earlier Jesus had said, 'No one can come to me unless the Father who sent me draws him' (6:44). Only Christ can set the sinner free: 'So if the Son sets you free, you will be free indeed' (8:36). Jesus spoke these words to the Jews, who were oppressed by the laws of their leaders (vv. 31–41). Thus, in the benediction, we praise God who 'has freed us from our sins by his blood' (Rev. 1:5). Christ's blood was the price paid to set us free (1 Peter 1:18–19).

HE MADE US A KINGDOM AND PRIESTS

Though we were once polluted by, and chained to, sin, we are now kings (NKJV) and priests. Terms used of Israel are now applied to the church (Exod. 19:6; 1 Peter 2:9).

We have been freed from the reign of sin and are now under the reign of grace: 'For sin shall not be your master, because you are not under law, but under grace' (Rom. 6:14). We ought to notice that this is a declaration of fact rather than a command. Christ has delivered us from the law's condemnation (Rom. 8:1, 31–34). Moreover, we reign over Satan, even now: 'Resist the devil, and he will flee from you' (James 4:7). We looked in a previous chapter at the promise which is also a benediction: 'The God of peace will soon crush Satan under your feet. The grace of our Lord Jesus be with you' (Rom. 16:20). Then our prayer will be answered: 'your kingdom come, your will be done on earth as it is in heaven' (Matt. 6:10). Meanwhile, while on earth we belong to God's kingdom 'that cannot be shaken' (Heb. 12:28). Christ the King cannot die or be defeated; his kingdom is everlasting and invincible.

In the Old Testament, priests came from only one nation: the Jewish race. They came from only one tribe: the Levites. They were only one gender: male. Only the high priest could enter the Most Holy Place, and even he could only go into that sacred place once a year, on the Day of Atonement, carrying the blood of a sacrificial animal (Lev. 16). Christians drawn from all nations, both men and women, have access to God all the time and at any time, both day and night. We may go confidently to God's throne, 'so that we may receive mercy and find grace to help us in our time of need' (Heb. 4:16).

What sacrifices do we offer? A broken heart (Ps. 51:17), a praying tongue (Ps. 141:2), a praising and a generous heart (Heb. 13:15–16) and a yielded life (Rom. 12:1–2). These are the sacrifices offered by the 'holy priesthood' that are 'acceptable to God through Jesus Christ' (1 Peter 2:5). This is how we 'serve [Christ's] God and Father' (Rev. 1:6). The church is God's temple, indwelt by the Holy Spirit, and all believers are priests (1 Cor. 6:19–20; 2 Cor. 6:16; Eph. 2:19–22).

In this benediction, we desire that the triune God will receive 'glory and power for ever and ever' (Rev. 1:6). How else could we respond when we realize what the triune God has done to save our immortal souls?

What Christ will do

We read in verse 7 four facts about Christ's second coming.

IT IS CERTAIN

'Look, he *is* coming' (emphasis added). Just before his death Jesus promised, 'I will come back and take you to be with me that you also may be where I am' (John 14:3). It is evident from the context that this promise was not just for the disciples who first heard the Saviour's words, but for all believers. He is preparing for them a place in his Father's house where there are 'many rooms'—there is room for all who trust him for salvation (14:1–4). The path to heaven is through Christ, who is the way, the truth and the life (14:6). Both Paul and Peter stress the certainty of Christ's coming: 'the Lord himself will come …' (1 Thes. 4:16); 'the day of the Lord will come …' (2 Peter 3:10).

IT WILL BE GLORIOUS

This is the meaning of the words 'he is coming with the clouds'. He who ascended into the clouds will come again out of the clouds (Luke 24:50–53; Acts 1:9–11; Matt. 24:30).

IT WILL BE VISIBLE

The words 'every eye will see him' indicate that Christ's return will not be like his ascension, seen only by a few; this event will be seen by everyone, the living and the dead, who will be summoned from their graves (John 5:28–29). Paul writes about this event to encourage the Thessalonians:

For the Lord himself will come down from heaven, with a loud command, with the voice of the archangel and with the trumpet call of God, and the dead in Christ will rise first. After that, we who are still alive and are left will be caught up together with them in the clouds to meet the Lord in the air. And so we will be with the Lord for ever.

(1 Thes. 4:16–17)

Everyone, believers and unbelievers, will know that Christ has come!

IT WILL CAUSE DISTRESS TO SOME AND JOY TO OTHERS

By writing 'even those who pierced him; and all the peoples of the earth will mourn because of him', John echoes Zechariah 12:10, which was partially fulfilled when Christ was nailed on the cross (John 19:37). Zechariah's prophecy will find its ultimate fulfilment when Christ comes a second time.

Unbelievers will mourn when they see Christ. The Jews who rejected him will see that Jesus of Nazareth, whom they crucified, is the promised Messiah and the only Saviour. This will be not the mourning of repentance but of hopelessness and despair. It is a mourning that will never end. When Christ comes, unbelievers will flee in terror from 'the wrath of the Lamb' (Rev. 6:15–17). However, in contrast to the misery of unbelievers, everlasting joy awaits those who are washed in the blood of the Lamb (1:5; 7:14).

Verse 7 ends with the affirmation 'So shall it be!' It shall be because God who planned Christ's first coming has also planned his second coming. The promises relating to his incarnation were fulfilled; so will be the promises of his second coming at the time predestined by God. What is our response? 'Amen'—'let it be!'

'Look, he is coming!' declares the apostle John. Are we eagerly looking for his return?

Notes

1 **Richard Brooks,** *The Lamb Is All the Glory: The Book of Revelation* (Welwyn Commentary; Welwyn: Evangelical Press, 1986), pp. 209–210.

2 There are four main schools of interpretation (with variations within each): Preterist—the events of the Revelation span the period from John until the Roman Emperor Constantine in the fourth century; Futurist—most of the prophecies are about the future; Historical—Revelation is a panorama of history from John until the end of the world; Spiritual (or Symbolic)—Revelation depicts the conflict between Christ and Satan (that even now Christ reigns in heaven, and history will reach its climax with the coming of the Lord Jesus Christ). The last is the interpretation of William Hendriksen and Richard Brooks. It is mine too!

3 **Hendriksen** lists some of the Old Testament passages quoted or alluded to in Revelation in *More Than Conquerors: An Interpretation of the Book of Revelation* (London: Inter-Varsity Press, 1962), p. 48.

4 Ibid., p. 55.

5 Ibid., p. 53.

6 **Hendriksen** takes verse 8 as Christ's words because the preceding and subsequent verses refer to Christ; ibid., p. 54. **Brooks** (*The Lamb Is All the Glory*) identifies God as the speaker, as does **Herman Hoeksema** in *Behold He Cometh: An Exposition of the Book of Revelation* (Grand Rapids, MI: Reformed Free Publishing Association, 1969), p. 29.

7 **Hoeksema,** *Behold He Cometh,* p. 29.

8 Ibid., pp. 29–30.

9 **Russell Brian,** *The Greatest Prayer Ever Prayed: A Devotional Exposition of John 17* (London: Grace Publications, 2010), p. 173.

10 **Brooks,** *The Lamb Is All the Glory,* p. 18.

11 **Hoeksema,** *Behold He Cometh,* p. 23.

The Creator on his throne (Rev. 4:8, 11)

Holy, holy, holy
is the Lord God Almighty,
who was, and is, and is to come ...
You are worthy, our Lord and God,
   to receive glory and honour and power,
for you created all things,
   and by your will they were created
   and have their being.

Revelation 4 depicts the throne room of the Creator God in heaven. The apostle John sees an open door and hears a voice that sounds like the blast of a trumpet (v. 1). The open door speaks of God's gracious invitation, and the trumpet indicates his command for sinners to enter his presence. In the Old Testament, the trumpet was often used to call people together to hear God's voice (as in Exod. 19:16–19). Besides the trumpet, the apostle hears twenty-four elders and four living creatures singing doxologies to 'the Lord God Almighty' who sits on his throne (v. 8).

The door

Is verse 1's 'door standing open' meant to remind us of Jacob's words after his dream at Bethel? The patriarch was running away from his angry brother Esau when he dreamed that 'he saw a stairway resting on the earth, with its top reaching to heaven, and the angels of God ...

ascending and descending on it' (Gen. 28:12). Above the ladder stood the Lord, who promised to give Jacob and his descendants the land on which Jacob was lying, a promise previously made to Jacob's grandfather, Abraham, and to his father, Isaac. God said, 'All peoples on earth will be blessed through you and your offspring' (28:14), and this promise was fulfilled through Jesus Christ, the Saviour of the world (John 4:42). Jacob declared, '... this [place] is none other than the house of God; this is the gate of heaven' (Gen. 28:17).

Jesus referred to Jacob's dream when he first met Nathanael: 'I tell you the truth, you shall see heaven open, and the angels of God ascending and descending on the Son of Man' (John 1:51). Jacob's ladder was a picture of Christ. Christ is the link between heaven and earth; it is through him that sinners may enter the throne room of the Creator God. His death reconciles sinners to the holy God. To change the metaphor, he is the door into God's presence, now and later (John 10:9).

The voice

Revelation 4:1–2 looks back to 1:10–13, where we read about 'a loud voice' calling John to 'Write on a scroll what you see'. This voice speaks again to John at 4:1; it is the voice of Christ. 'I turned around to see the voice that was speaking to me. And when I turned I saw seven golden lampstands, and among the lampstands was someone "like a son of man"' (1:12–13). The seven lampstands are the seven churches of Asia; it is Christ who walks among the churches (1:20). 'It had been more than sixty years since he heard that voice, but it was as familiar to him as it had been in his youth. It was the voice of his Beloved.'[1] What does the voice say? 'Come up here, and I will show you what must take place after this' (4:1). The word 'must' assures the apostle—and us—that, despite persecution, no person, however mighty or evil, can overthrow the decrees of Almighty God.

The throne

After seeing the open door and hearing the voice, the apostle John sees a throne. The word 'throne' occurs sixteen times in Revelation 4–5. John says he 'was in the Spirit' when he saw this throne (v. 2). The Holy Spirit lifts John from his surroundings so that he is wholly absorbed with the things that he sees.

Who is sitting on this throne? The question is answered in verse 8: 'the Lord God Almighty'. Believers have 'little strength' (3:8), but God is the Almighty (4:8). The message of the throne is that God reigns.

As John looked at the throne he saw that 'the one who sat there had the appearance of jasper and carnelian. A rainbow, resembling an emerald, encircled the throne' (v. 3). The words 'appearance' and 'resembling' remind us that this was a vision; what the apostle saw were symbols that tell us something about the character of God.

- *Jasper*: 'This is a transparent stone, rather like a diamond … which offers to the eye a variety of most vivid colours … it signifies to us the glorious and infinite perfection of God, and especially the purity and dazzling brightness of His holiness.'[2]
- *Carnelian*, also known as sardius, is similar to a ruby and blood-red in colour. This red stone speaks to us of God's justice and wrath.
- *Emerald:* the restful green emerald denotes God's peace that comes to us through Christ because of his death at Calvary (Rom. 5:1–2).

These three precious stones representing God's holiness, God's wrath and God's peace sum up the gospel.

Around God's throne is a 'rainbow, resembling an emerald' (v. 3). The rainbow recalls the story of Noah and the sign of God's promise never to flood the world again (Gen. 9:8–17). It speaks of God's covenant. The holy God on the throne delights to pardon sinners. In contrast to the sight of the colourful rainbow—the emblem of God's mercy—John also sees 'flashes of lightning' and hears 'rumblings and peals of thunder'—the emblems of God's wrath (v. 5).

Moses and the Israelites also saw and heard 'thunder and lightning, with a thick cloud over the mountain, and a very loud trumpet blast' (Exod. 19:16–19) prior to God giving the Ten Commandments at Mount Sinai (Exod. 20:1–17). Then followed more thunder. Moses wrote,

When the people saw the thunder and lightning and heard the trumpet and saw the mountain in smoke, they trembled with fear. They stayed at a distance and said to Moses, 'Speak to us yourself and we will listen. But do not have God speak to us or we will die.' Moses said to the people, 'Do not be afraid. God has come to test you, so that the fear of God will be with you to keep you from sinning.' The people remained at a distance, while Moses approached the thick darkness where God was.

(Exod. 20:18–21)

We, like Israel, have broken God's commands, and, like Israel, deserve the storm of his wrath to burst upon us. However, just as Moses became the mediator between the holy God and the sinful Israelites, so Christ became the Mediator between God and ourselves. God's wrath fell on Christ instead of us, even though he had lived a sinless life. He died the death that we deserve.

Awestruck, John saw that 'Before the throne, seven lamps were blazing. These are the seven spirits[3] of God' (Rev. 4:5). The Holy Spirit, who came like fire at Pentecost (Acts 2:3), burns up sin in the hearts of believers and pours out the fire of God's anger on the unrepentant.

What is the significance of the 'sea of glass, clear as crystal', before the throne (v. 6)? Is this a reference to the laver—the basin of water—in the tabernacle? The priests washed in the laver before entering the Holy Place (Exod. 30:17–21). We must be washed in Christ's blood before we approach God's throne. Moreover, the sea reflects 'the Lord God Almighty' sitting on his throne; we too should reflect God's glory by our holy living, until we perfectly reflect his glory in heaven.

The twenty-four thrones

Who are the twenty-four elders who sit on twenty-four thrones around God's throne? I agree with the explanation of Brooks: 'Simple mathematics reminds us that 24 is made up of 12+12, and Bible knowledge teaches us that there were twelve tribes of Israel and twelve apostles in the New Testament. So these twenty-four elders stand symbolically as representatives of the whole church of God throughout the old and new dispensations.'[4]

The elders are 'dressed in white' (4:4; 7:13–15) because they have been washed in Christ's blood and are now completely sanctified; they have 'crowns of gold on their heads' because they are rewarded for their faithfulness to Christ in the 'good fight' (2 Tim. 4:7). 'They lay their crowns before the throne' (v. 10) because God alone is worthy of praise (v. 11). The elders—the whole church of God—delight to worship the everlasting God, 'who lives for ever and ever' (v. 10). Can John see any empty thrones? Not at all! Every seat is filled; not one of God's elect is missing.

Before we move on, let's pause and think about the significance of the final words of verse 10: 'They lay their crowns before the throne.' These words demonstrate that we are saved by God's grace alone; we are not worthy of the least honour in the presence of God.

The four living creatures

Who are these mysterious creatures who worship God 'Day and night' (vv. 6–8)? Comparing Revelation 4 with Ezekiel 1 and 10, we may conclude that these 'living creatures' are the cherubim, one of the highest orders of angels.[5] Their song in verse 8 is similar to that of the six-winged seraphs (angelic beings distinct from the cherubim) that Isaiah heard (Isa. 6:1–3).

There are four of these living creatures, representing the four compass points—the four corners of the world—indicating that they are ready to serve God wherever he sends them. Each creature is covered with eyes, 'even under his wings' (vv. 6, 8). Each creature has a different appearance: 'The first living creature was like a lion, the second was like an ox, the third had a face like a man, the fourth was like a flying eagle' (v. 7). Hendriksen explains these facets of the living creatures: they are 'in strength like the lion, in ability to render service like the ox, in intelligence like man—notice also their many eyes, indicating intellectual perception—and in swiftness like the eagle, ever ready to obey God's commandments'.[6] We too ought to be swift to serve God, whatever the task and wherever he sends us.

The songs

The four living creatures and the twenty-four elders unceasingly worship God: 'Day and night they never stop … Whenever the living creatures give glory, honour and thanks to him who sits on the throne … the twenty-four elders fall down … and worship him who lives for ever and ever' (vv. 8–10). They are never bored; they are never tired; they delight in, and live only for, the adoration of God.

To whom is their praise given? To the three-in-one God: the Father who sits on his throne, the Son who is seen in the symbolism of the crystal sea, and the Spirit who is depicted as the seven blazing lamps. Here again is the tri-unity of God, a motif that occurs in so many biblical benedictions and doxologies.

The angels and the church focus on four attributes of the triune God.

GOD IS HOLY

'Holy, holy, holy' (v. 8). God is separate from and exalted above his creation; all that he does is pure and perfect; he is majestic and glorious. Is the repetition of the word 'holy' an indication that each Person of the Trinity is holy? Jonathan Edwards says, 'Holiness is more than a mere attribute of God—it is the sum of all his attributes, the outshining of all that God is.'[7] It is because God is holy that he hates sin and will punish sinners. How amazing that this holy God saves sinners!

GOD IS ALMIGHTY

'Lord God Almighty' (v. 8). The elders praise the Almighty as the Creator: '... you created all things, and by your will they were created and have their being' (v. 11). God simply spoke and a perfect world was created in six days (Gen. 1:1–31; notice the refrain 'And God said ...' and the phrase 'it was very good' in v. 31).[8]

GOD IS SOVEREIGN

It was by God's will—his eternal decree—that the world was made. Nothing happens apart from 'the plan of him who works out everything in conformity with the purpose of his will' (Eph. 1:11). The 'great multitude' of the redeemed in heaven will sing, 'Hallelujah! For our Lord God Almighty reigns' (Rev. 19:6). He reigns now! We adore the Almighty even now while still on earth. How much better we will praise him with sinless souls in glorified bodies!

GOD IS EVERLASTING

'... who was, and is, and is to come' (v. 8; 1:4, 8). God had no beginning; he has no end. He will never cease to exist. The eternal God is unchanging in his love towards his people; there is nothing, and no one, that can separate us from his love that comes to us through the Lord Jesus Christ (Rom. 8:28–39).

This God is worthy 'to receive glory and honour and power' (v. 11). He alone is worthy to receive such adoration not only from our lips, but also from lives dedicated to him. We ought to notice the word 'our' in verse 11. We, though unworthy, can call the almighty God, worshipped by cherubim and seraphim, 'our Lord and God'! He is ours because of sovereign grace and unfathomable love.

Chapter 25

Notes

1 **Donald Fortner,** *Discovering Christ in Revelation* (Darlington: Evangelical Press, 2002), p. 55.
2 **Richard Brooks,** *The Lamb Is All the Glory: The Book of Revelation* (Welwyn Commentary; Welwyn: Evangelical Press, 1986), p. 56.
3 See my comments on 'the seven spirits' in Ch. 24.
4 **Brooks,** *The Lamb Is All the Glory*, p. 56.
5 There are sixty-two references to cherubim in the Old Testament (e.g. Gen. 3:24; Exod. 25:17–22; 1 Kings 6:23–35; Ps. 18:10), but only one mention in the New Testament (Heb. 9:5). Seraphs (or seraphim, NKJV) appear only once in the Bible (Isa. 6:1–3). To understand more about angels read **Roger Ellsworth,** *What the Bible Teaches about Angels* (Darlington: Evangelical Press, 2005). **Hendriksen** compares the 'living ones' in Ezekiel with 'the living creatures' in Revelation in *More Than Conquerors: An Interpretation of the Book of Revelation* (London: Inter-Varsity Press, 1962), pp. 86–87.
6 **Hendriksen,** *More Than Conquerors*, p. 87.
7 Quoted in **Brooks,** *The Lamb Is All the Glory*, p. 59.
8 See Psalms 19:1–6; 24:1–2; 33:6, 9; 104:1–35.

The Lamb and the scroll (Rev. 5:12–13)

Worthy is the Lamb, who was slain,
to receive power and wealth and wisdom and strength
and honour and glory and praise! ...
To him who sits on the throne and to the Lamb
be praise and honour and glory and power
for ever and ever!

What a scene: 'thousands upon thousands, and ten thousand times ten thousand', with the 'living creatures' (the cherubim) and 'the elders' (the entire number of the redeemed) singing in harmony with 'a loud voice', 'Worthy is the Lamb, who was slain'! Soon they are joined by 'every creature in heaven and on earth and under the sea', singing praise to 'him who sits on the throne and to the Lamb'! This is what John, the exiled apostle, heard. What a wonderful benediction for believers to hear at the end of a service of worship!

To understand fully the doxologies of verses 12–13 we must set them in the context of Revelation 5, in which we read about the scroll (vv. 1–5), the Saviour (vv. 5–7) and the songs (vv. 8–14).

The scroll

John sees a scroll in God's right hand, entirely covered with writing on both sides. A scroll was a long piece of papyrus or animal skin, rolled from both ends into the middle. This scroll represents God's plan from eternity past into eternity future. At the centre of this plan is the salvation of his elect through Christ's death at Calvary. God's right hand indicates his power and authority. History is not a haphazard series of events; rather, it is moving forward, according to what God has predestined, towards the glorious return of the Lord Jesus Christ. Meanwhile, the wise God plans everything for the good of his people to enhance his glory (Rom. 8:28). The hand that was nailed to the cross unfolds the events of our lives with wisdom and love.

This scroll is sealed with seven seals (v. 1). Seven is the number of perfection and completeness because God rested on the seventh day after creating a perfect world. God's work in creation, providence (his ruling of the universe and his care of his people) and salvation is always perfect.

A 'mighty angel' proclaims with a loud voice, so that the whole universe can hear, 'Who is worthy to break the seals and open the scroll?' (v. 2). There is 'no one in heaven' (angels or departed saints) or 'on earth' (saved or unsaved) or 'under the earth' (Satan and fallen angels) who 'could open the scroll or even look inside it' (v. 3). No one can fathom or fulfil God's plan to save sinners. A closed scroll would mean that God's plan would remain unfulfilled; this fact brings uncontrollable tears to John's eyes (v. 4). Christ is the only one who can unlock the scroll; he is the only Mediator between depraved sinners and the holy God.

The Saviour

'Do not weep! See …,' commands an elder (v. 5). The word 'see' means 'look attentively and be amazed at what you see'. What does the elder command John to see?

'THE LION OF THE TRIBE OF JUDAH' (V. 5)

This title has its roots in aged Jacob's prophecy concerning the descendants of his son Judah:

You are a lion's cub, O Judah;
>   you return from the prey, my son.
Like a lion he crouches and lies down,
>   like a lioness—who dares to rouse him?
The sceptre will not depart from Judah,
>   nor the ruler's staff from between his feet,
until he comes to whom it belongs
>   and the obedience of the nations is his.   (Gen. 49:9–10)

The lion was the king of beasts and renowned for strength, an appropriate type of Christ, the mighty Lion who triumphed at the cross over Satan, the roaring lion (Col. 2:15; 1 Peter 5:8). The divine lion chains the roaring lion.

THE 'ROOT OF DAVID' (V. 5)

This is a metaphor drawn from the prophecies of Isaiah (4:2; 11:1; 53:2), Jeremiah (23:5–6; 33:15–16) and Zechariah (3:8; 6:12). Christ came from the royal family of David (Rom. 1:3), the second king of Israel, which in the first century AD was like a decayed tree with only a stump left. Christ brought the tree alive! He is the Branch of whom the prophets spoke. He fulfilled their prophecies about Messiah's birth, life, death, resurrection and ascension. He is the King greater than David, whose reign is everlasting; the sovereign who will never die, nor lose his kingdom.

A 'LAMB, LOOKING AS IF IT HAD BEEN SLAIN' (V. 6)

John expects to see a lion but he sees a lamb! The mighty Lion is also the meek Lamb. The Lamb who died to save his people is also the Lion who defends them!

The slain Lamb is another image lifted from the pages of the Old Testament. Just as the Passover lamb died instead of the Israelites' firstborn sons, so Christ, our Passover Lamb, died in the place of God's sons; Jews and non-Jews who repent of their sins are God's firstborn (Exod. 12; 1 Cor. 5:7; Heb. 12:22–24). The Lamb, who was God in human flesh, silently allowed himself to be led to the slaughter to die for his lost sheep (Isa. 53:6–7; Luke 15:1–7). Do the words 'as if it had been slain' signify that Christ's human body in heaven still bears the marks of the nails that were driven into his hands and feet?

The Lamb has 'seven horns and seven eyes, which are the seven spirits of God sent out into all the world' (v. 6). He is the all-powerful ('seven horns') and all-seeing ('seven eyes') Lamb, who, after his death and resurrection, ascended into heaven and sent his Holy Spirit, represented by the 'seven spirits'. The Holy Spirit empowers the church to preach the gospel throughout the world (Acts 1:8).

We read that the Lamb 'came and took the scroll from the right hand of him who sat on the throne' (v. 7). Taking the scroll emphasizes Christ's willing acceptance of God's plan. David, in Psalm 40, places in Messiah's mouth these words: 'Then I said, "Here I am, I have come—it is written about me in the scroll. I desire to do your will, O my God; your law is within my heart"' (vv. 7–8). The writer to the Hebrews confirms that this prophecy relates to Jesus the Messiah (Heb. 10:5–7). Christ willingly carried out God's will.

The response of the cherubim and the elders to the Lamb taking the scroll is to fall 'down before the Lamb. Each one had a harp and they were holding golden bowls full of incense, which are the prayers of the saints' (v. 8). Why are we so slow to pray when God esteems our prayers a delightful fragrance? It is through prayer that, even while on earth, we enter the open door in heaven (4:1). And it is through prayer that we reign (5:10; compare 8:3–4)—the almighty God fulfils some of his plans through our prayers! Isn't that amazing? The harps and the bowls mean that all that the prophets prophesied and all the prayers that the believers prayed will be finally fulfilled.

The songs

We now listen to three songs: that of the living creatures (the cherubim) and the elders (the church) in verses 8–10, and those in which the angels (in vv. 11–12) and all creation (in v. 13) join in. A moment before there was silence (v. 3); now there is a crescendo of praise (vv. 9–14).

The song of the angels and the redeemed is 'a new song' (v. 9) because 'never before had such a great and glorious deliverance been accomplished and never before had the Lamb received this great honour'.[1] The theme of this song is that the Lamb's blood has 'purchased men for God' (v. 9). Christ's blood is the precious price paid to appease God and to set sinners free (1 Peter 1:18–19).

The redeemed will come 'from every tribe and language and people and nation' (v. 9; see also 7:9). All will understand one another; the curse of Babel will be reversed (Gen. 11:1–9). The Day of Pentecost, when 'each one heard them speaking in his own language … declaring the wonders of God' (Acts 2:8, 11), was a foretaste of the future. We won't need interpreters and translators in heaven!

The redeemed are, even now, 'a kingdom and priests to serve our God' (v. 10). We are kings and priests who have complete access to God, who accepts our worship and our service. We 'will reign on the earth', that is, on 'a new earth'—the final home of God's people (Rev. 21:1–3; 2 Peter 3:13; compare Isa. 65:17–25; 66:22). Heaven will be on earth. Then, Scriptures such as Isaiah 11:9 and Habakkuk 2:14 will be fulfilled: 'the earth will be full of the knowledge of the LORD as the waters cover the sea.'

The sevenfold doxology of verse 12 and the fourfold doxology of verse 13 express the highest adoration that we can offer to God's eternal Son, the Lord Jesus Christ, the Lamb and the Redeemer. One day, the church militant on earth will become the church triumphant in heaven, and then we will sing praise 'To him who sits on the throne and to the Lamb … for ever and ever!' (v. 13). Endless blessing, endless honour, endless praise, endless glory and endless worship belong to God the Father and the Lord Jesus Christ. The creation is unable to contain its joy over its imminent redemption (see Rom. 8:19–22).

The word 'wealth' (v. 12), which is translated as 'riches' in the NKJV, may seem out of place in this song of praise. Several Scriptures throw light on this description of Christ. Take, for example, 2 Corinthians 8:9: 'For you know the grace of our Lord Jesus Christ, that though he was rich, yet for your sakes he became poor, so that you through his poverty might become rich' (compare Phil. 2:5–11). In his letter to the Ephesians, Paul wrote about the cluster of spiritual blessings that we receive from Christ (1:3–14). These are 'the riches of God's grace that he lavished on us' (Eph. 1:7–8). The God who is 'rich in mercy' has lifted us into 'the heavenly realms in Christ Jesus' (2:4, 6).

What response can we make as we consider the Creator on his throne (Rev. 4) and the Lamb who opened the scroll (Rev. 5)? We declare, with the cherubim, 'Amen' (5:14). This 'Amen' is 'not a faint little murmur that can scarcely be heard, but a sound like claps of thunder, an expression of confident faith and glad worship, a thorough assent to all that has been said—a cry of "This is so! This is gloriously true!"'[2] What can we do but fall down, with the elders, and worship the triune God (v. 14)?

Notes

1 **William Hendriksen,** *More Than Conquerors: An Interpretation of the Book of Revelation* (London: Inter-Varsity Press, 1962), p. 91.

2 **Richard Brooks,** *The Lamb Is All the Glory: The Book of Revelation* (Welwyn Commentary; Welwyn: Evangelical Press, 1986), p. 69.

God reigns!
(Rev. 11:15–19; 19:1–10)

… our Lord and … his Christ,

… will reign for ever and ever …

We give thanks to you, Lord God Almighty,

    the One who is and who was,

because you have taken your great power

    and have begun to reign …

Hallelujah!

Salvation and glory and power belong to our God …

Hallelujah!

    For our Lord God Almighty reigns.

Let us rejoice and be glad

    and give him glory!

For the wedding of the Lamb has come,

    and his bride has made herself ready.

T he book of Revelation overflows with songs of praise. We would expect to hear a doxology when the elect from all the races of the world are delivered out of tribulation (7:11–17). God protects his people (end of 7:15) and wipes every tear from their eyes (7:17). The Lamb, who is also their Shepherd, leads 'them to springs of living water'—at last they are fully satisfied and completely holy, resting like contented sheep in the Good Shepherd's presence. Doxology is appropriate: 'Amen! Praise and glory and wisdom and thanks and honour and power and strength be to our God for ever and ever. Amen!' (7:12).

On the other hand, we might, in subsequent chapters of Revelation, feel uncomfortable to read doxologies when God destroys his enemies. There are four passages in which God is praised for the punishment of the wicked (11:15–19; 15:1–4; 16:4–7; 19:1–10). We will zoom in on two of these passages.

Revelation 11:15–19

We must read these verses in their context to understand them fully. The seven seals of chapters 6–8, which describe 'not only persecution, but every form of trial and tribulation',[1] are opened alongside the blowing of the seven trumpets of judgement in chapters 8–11. The trumpets 'do not symbolize single and separate events, but they refer to woes that may be seen any day of the year in any part of the globe. Therefore, the trumpets are synchronous with the seals.'[2] These judgements, though similar to the ten plagues in Egypt (Exod. 7–11), are far worse and anticipate the final day of judgement.

Who are the two witnesses (11:1–14)? They are not actual men but a symbol of the church speaking about Christ; we speak of a Saviour we know. Why two? The law demanded two witnesses to establish the truth (Deut. 17:6; 19:15). Christ sent seventy of his disciples two by two to declare his Word (Luke 10:1).

The symbolism of measuring the temple (11:1–2) relates to the nature of the church, whereas the picture of the two witnesses deals with the task of the church. These illustrations teach us about the true character of the church, God's temple, and the mission of the church until Christ returns. This chapter draws on the imagery of the Old Testament in passages such as Zechariah 4 and also refers to the prayers of Elijah (1 Kings 17; James 5:17–18).

The world rebels against God, despite his judgements, and rejects the witness of his church; therefore, the seventh trumpet sounds to call the recalcitrant to judgement (11:15). The 'loud voices' are probably those of angels rejoicing because 'The kingdom of the world has become the kingdom of our Lord and of his Christ, and he will reign for ever and ever' (v. 15). Christ reigns now, 'but once the judgement day has arrived, the full royal splendour of God's sovereignty will be revealed, for all opposition will then be abolished'.³ Praise, rather than tears, fills heaven because God's glory is declared and displayed.

The church, represented by the twenty-four elders, knew that the sovereign God would overthrow the wicked but the reality of this event overwhelms them, so that they prostrate themselves in adoration (v. 16). No longer do angels or the church worship the God 'who is to come', as at 1:8 and 4:8, because he has come in 'great power' to 'reign' (v. 17). Angels and the redeemed 'give thanks' to God because he will punish the sinful and compensate the righteous; good and bad will stand before the Almighty (v. 18).

The phrases 'The nations were angry' and 'your wrath has come' (v. 18) are reminiscent of Psalm 2:

Why do the nations conspire
    and the peoples plot in vain?
The kings of the earth take their stand
    and the rulers gather together
against the LORD
    and against his Anointed One.   (vv. 1–2)

The title 'Christ' means anointed. However, as Psalm 2 continues,

The One enthroned in heaven laughs;
    the Lord scoffs at them.
Then he rebukes them in his anger
    and terrifies them in his wrath.   (vv. 4–5)

'The time has come for judging the dead' (Rev. 11:18) reiterates Jesus's solemn prediction in John 5:28–29: 'Do not be amazed at this [the judgement], for a time is coming when all who are in their graves will hear his voice and come out—those who have done good will rise to live, and those who have done evil will rise to be condemned.'

It is interesting to notice the various groups specified in Revelation 11:18.

- *'Your servants the prophets'* are the men, such as Jeremiah and Isaiah, who faithfully declared God's Word even though verbally abused and physically persecuted. Like Moses, they did not fear the wrath of human rulers and religious leaders, because they feared 'him who is invisible' (Heb. 11:27).
- *'Your saints'*: God views his people while still on earth as saints (e.g. Phil. 1:1) because they are covered with the robe of Christ's righteousness (Isa. 61:10). One day, the saints will have not only the title but also the character of saints. The 'pure in heart'—pure means sincere—will then become sinless when they see God (Matt. 5:8; 1 John 3:1–3).
- The saints are those *'who reverence your name'* (compare 19:5). Awe of God is not incompatible with inexpressible joy. The believer's highest joy is to adore God!
- *'Small and great'* (occurs again at 19:5). Brooks's comments are encouraging: 'Not just the greats of evangelical church history, but the "common people" among God's flock, the silent and unthanked labourers, the unknown servants of God who plodded on faithfully, the weak and timid ones, the children who loved their Redeemer and their teachers who taught them of Him, the godly parents who sought amidst much trial and heartache and disappointment to train up their children in the way of the Lord and to honour God in their families. Not one missing. Not one forgotten.'4

God's temple open in heaven (11:19) speaks of access—even now—to

God. The 'ark of his covenant' was the small box inside the Most Holy Place into which the high priest went once a year with sacrificial blood. An animal was killed instead of the sinner; its blood was sprinkled on the lid, known as the atonement cover (or mercy seat, NKJV); thus God's wrath was appeased. Christ, the Lamb of God, died in our place; he is our mercy seat: his blood reconciles us to God.

Revelation 19:1–10

This crescendo of praise follows the destruction of 'the great prostitute' (v. 2), whose vile portrait is unmasked in the previous two chapters (see also 14:8; 16:19). This prostitute wears on her forehead the title

MYSTERY

BABYLON THE GREAT

THE MOTHER OF PROSTITUTES

AND OF THE ABOMINATIONS

OF THE EARTH   (17:5)

What does this prostitute-city represent? Hendriksen explains: the term prostitute 'indicates that which allures, tempts, seduces and draws people away from God'; a city 'reminds us of pleasure-mad, arrogant, presumptuous Babylon of old', and of first-century Rome (a city built on seven hills, 17:9). Therefore, Babylon 'symbolizes the concentration of the luxury, vice and glamour of this world' that is opposed to, and seeks to entice, the church—believers—to unfaithfulness to Christ, the divine bridegroom (2 Cor. 11:1–3).[5]

John, in his first epistle, had already warned the church about this dangerous prostitute-city:

Do not love the world or anything in the world. If anyone loves the world, the love of the Father is not in him. For everything in the world—the cravings of sinful man, the lust of his eyes and the boasting of what he has and does—comes not from the Father but from the world. The world and its desires pass away, but the man who does the will of God lives for ever.

(1 John 2:15–17)

The message of Revelation 17–19 is that God will destroy this beguiling world!

John hears 'what sounded like the roar of a great multitude in heaven shouting: "Hallelujah!"' (19:1). Similar terms are used in verse 6. 'Imagine all the oceans and mighty waterfalls, all the choirs and all the thunders of the world, going strong at the same time, and even then you are only just beginning to imagine a fraction of what those paeans of worship and praise to God will sound like at the Last Day!'[6]

God is praised for 'Salvation', which comes from him alone, for the 'glory and power' that belong to him alone (v. 1), and for his justice in punishing the wicked, whose sins deserve his wrath (v. 2). The wicked are not annihilated, nor do they suffer for no more than a brief time; they are punished 'for ever and ever' (v. 3). Jesus taught that the joy of heaven is never-ending, and so is the misery of hell: 'Then they [unbelievers] will go away to eternal punishment, but the righteous to eternal life' (Matt. 25:46). The salvation of his people and the banishment of his enemies from his awesome presence (2 Thes. 1:7–10) cause those in heaven to proclaim that 'our Lord God Almighty reigns' (Rev. 19:6). Both the salvation of his people and the punishment of his enemies enhance his glory.

God takes 'no pleasure in the death of the wicked'; rather, he desires that they should 'turn from their ways and live'. His appeal to sinners is 'Turn! Turn from your evil ways! Why will you die?' (Ezek. 33:11). Nevertheless, because he is holy and just, 'the wicked man' who does not repent 'will die for his sin' (vv. 8–9). Tragically, the sinner reaps the consequences of his or her obduracy. It is the duty, and ought to be the delight, of believers to earnestly urge unbelievers to repent (2 Cor. 5:19–

20). The eighteenth-century evangelist George Whitefield preached about hell with tears flowing from his eyes—and so should we.

Angels and the redeemed extol God not only for the overthrow of the ungodly, but also because of 'the wedding of the Lamb' (19:7). Whoever heard of attending the wedding of a Lamb! John the Baptist identified the Bridegroom-Lamb as the Lord Jesus Christ (John 1:29; 3:27–30). The 'Lamb', as a title for Christ, occurs thirty-two times in the NIV translation of the book of Revelation.[7] The metaphor of the Lamb looks back to Old Testament passages such as Exodus 12 and Isaiah 53.

Who is the 'bride' of the Lamb (19:7)? An angel says to John, 'Come, I will show you the bride, the wife of the Lamb', before he carries the apostle to 'a mountain great and high', where he sees 'the Holy City, Jerusalem, coming down out of heaven from God. It shone with the glory of God, and its brilliance was like that of a very precious jewel' (21:9–12; see also vv. 2–3). It is clear from these verses that the Holy City is not a place but people, Christ's bride for whom he shed his blood on the cross (Eph. 5:25).

The bride's wedding dress is 'Fine linen, bright and clean' (19:8). Having been washed from sin by Christ's blood (1:5, NKJV; 7:14; 1 John 1:7), she prepares for the wedding, when the Bridegroom will come, by holy living: 'Fine linen stands for the righteous acts of the saints' (19:8). Notice the word 'given' in verse 8: salvation is God's gift, as is the desire and ability to live a sanctified life. We lead holy lives as we apply the teaching of God's holy Word—his Word is like soap (Eph. 5:25–27)! 'Fine linen' indicates that 'we shall be arrayed completely, head to foot, in Christ's righteousness, covered through and through with the beauty of holiness'.[8]

God sends an angel, who says, 'Write: "Blessed are those who are invited to the wedding supper of the Lamb!"' And he adds, 'These are the true words of God' (19:9). We are indeed 'blessed' ('to be envied', Amplified Bible)—to receive an invitation to the Lamb's wedding. This wedding invitation is the free offer of the gospel that comes to us by the Holy Spirit through gospel preaching and evangelistic activity (represented by the two witnesses in ch. 11). 'The Holy Spirit and the bride say, "Come!"' (22:17). Have you come? Have you received God's gracious invitation?

John is so overcome with emotion that he falls at the feet of the angel to worship him (19:10). The angel commands the apostle, 'Worship God!'—he alone is worthy of our adoration.

Notes

1 **William Hendriksen,** *More Than Conquerors: An Interpretation of the Book of Revelation* (London: Inter-Varsity Press, 1962), p. 115.

2 Ibid., p. 116.

3 Ibid., p. 132.

4 **Richard Brooks,** *The Lamb Is All the Glory: The Book of Revelation* (Welwyn Commentary; Welwyn: Evangelical Press, 1986), p. 115.

5 **Hendriksen,** *More Than Conquerors*, pp. 167–168.

6 **Brooks,** *The Lamb Is All the Glory*, p. 160.

7 See 5:6, 8, 12–13; 6:1, 3, 5, 7, 16; 7:9–10, 14, 17; 12:11; 13:8, 11; 14:1, 4, 10; 15:3; 17:14; 19:7, 9; 21:9, 14, 22–23, 27; 22:1, 3.

8 **Brooks,** *The Lamb Is All the Glory*, p. 163.

Come, Lord Jesus
(Rev. 22:20–21)

He who testifies to these things says, 'Yes, I am coming soon.'
Amen. Come, Lord Jesus.
The grace of the Lord Jesus be with God's people. Amen.

The Bible reaches its climax with a two-verse benediction that focuses on the second coming of the Lord Jesus Christ. Three questions will enable us to think about this grand finale of world history.

Who is coming?
It is Christ who says three times in this final chapter, 'I am coming' (v. 7, 12, 20). There are several descriptions of him in Revelation 22.

THE 'LAMB'
The apostle John sees 'the river of the water of life ... flowing from the throne of God and of the Lamb' (v. 1) which is 'in the city' (v. 3). The city is the church, the radiant bride of the enthroned Lamb: 'I saw the Holy City, the new Jerusalem, coming down out of heaven from God, prepared as a bride beautifully dressed for her husband' (21:2). God will live with his people for ever on 'a new earth'; heaven will be on earth (21:1). What is 'the water of life'? The term indicates 'the gloriously satisfying and God-given life of the church of God in glory'.[1]

In Revelation 5 we read about the Lamb who was slain in the place of believers (v. 6), and in Revelation 6 we read about the Lamb who will slay unbelievers when he comes again. Unbelievers, from the greatest to the least, will call 'to the mountains and the rocks, "Fall on us and hide us from the face of him who sits on the throne and from the wrath of the Lamb!"' (6:16). It is only those who are washed 'in the blood of the Lamb' (7:14) who will escape his wrath and enter heaven.

Christ is both a Lamb and a Shepherd in heaven: 'For the Lamb at the centre of the throne will be their shepherd; he will lead them to springs of living water. And God will wipe away every tear from their eyes' (7:17; see also Isa. 25:8).

THE 'ALPHA AND THE OMEGA, THE FIRST AND THE LAST, THE BEGINNING AND THE END'

This description is found at 22:13 (see also 1:8; 21:6). Alpha and Omega are the first and last letters of the Greek alphabet. It is in Christ, God the Son, that we see who God is and what he is like. He is the perfect and complete revelation of God. In the first chapter of Revelation, God is called 'the Alpha and the Omega' (1:4); in the last chapter this title is given to Christ to affirm his deity.

THE 'ROOT AND THE OFFSPRING OF DAVID'

This title, from 22:16, was also used at 5:5 and means that 'Christ is the promised Messiah, God's own Son. He is the royal King to whom is given all power and authority in heaven and earth. He is our divine and human Saviour.'[2]

THE 'BRIGHT MORNING STAR'

This phrase, also in verse 16 (compare 2:28; 2 Peter 1:19), is drawn from Numbers 24:17: 'A star will come out of Jacob; a sceptre will rise out of Israel.' 'Christ Himself is coming, and that coming heralds the dawn of everlasting day when He will give Himself to His people and share His glory with them in a way which at present is utterly beyond our imagination.'[3] At this point it is worth noting the following verses:

I consider that our present sufferings are not worth comparing with the glory that will be revealed in us. (Rom. 8:18)

When Christ, who is your life, appears, then you also will appear with him in glory. (Col. 3:4)

… on the day he [Christ] comes to be glorified in his holy people and to be marvelled at among all those who have believed. This includes you, because you believed our testimony to you. (2 Thes. 1:10)

Christ will be 'glorified in his holy people'—this is something to eagerly look forward to!

How is Christ coming?

His coming will be …

PERSONAL

Jesus says, '*I* am coming' (vv. 7, 12, 20, emphasis added). The angels, at Christ's ascension, said to the sky-gazing disciples, 'This same Jesus, who has been taken from you into heaven, will come back in the same way you have seen him go into heaven' (Acts 1:11).

CERTAIN

Jesus says, 'He who testifies to these things says, "Yes, I am coming soon"' (v. 20). 'He who testifies' means, 'What I say is the truth. I am God, who cannot lie.' The word 'Yes' signifies that no event, nor any person, human or demonic, can say 'no' to what Christ has planned and promised.

SOON

Jesus says, 'I am coming *soon*' (vv. 7, 12, 20, emphasis added). Was

Jesus mistaken? Over two thousand years have elapsed since his promise. The emphasis of this word is not on the time of his return but on the suddenness of that event. Just as the people in the days of Noah were unprepared and surprised by the Flood, so unbelievers will be unprepared and surprised when Christ returns (Matt. 24:36–40). Noah, 'a preacher of righteousness', warned those who sneered at his ark-building and his prediction of coming judgement; they would not believe (2 Peter 2:5). Likewise, Christians warn sinners about Christ's coming—and they also will not believe. Christ's coming will catch unbelievers as unprepared as they are for the coming of a thief (Matt. 24:42–44). 'Get ready by repentance' is the message of this word 'soon'.

How should we prepare for Christ's coming?

His return, which will terrify unbelievers, ought not to surprise believers; rather, we ought always to be ready to welcome our coming Lord and Saviour. How do we prepare for Christ's coming?

REPENTANCE

The gracious invitation in verse 17 answers the question: 'The Spirit and the bride say, "Come!" And let him who hears say, "Come!" Whoever is thirsty, let him come; and whoever wishes, let him take the free gift of the water of life.' God the Holy Spirit and the church—'the bride'—call sinners to come in repentance to the Lamb.

We are to come to Christ as a thirsty person comes to drink water. Seeking God is often compared to the thirsty urgently looking for water. Take two examples from the Psalms:

O God, you are my God,
>   earnestly I seek you;
my soul thirsts for you,

my body longs for you,
in a dry and weary land
    where there is no water.   (Ps. 63:1)

As the deer pants for streams of water,
    so my soul pants for you, O God.
My soul thirsts for God, for the living God.   (Ps. 42:1–2)

In a desert without water, a man or an animal will die! Is this how we thirst for God? Christ is 'the water of life' to those who are spiritually thirsty.

This invitation, '"Come!" Whoever is thirsty …' is reminiscent of Jesus's conversation with the woman of Samaria (John 4:1–26) and his words in Jerusalem about the Holy Spirit: '"If anyone is thirsty, let him come to me and drink. Whoever believes in me, as the Scripture has said, streams of living water will flow from within him." By this he meant the Spirit, whom those who believed in him were later to receive' (John 7:37–39). Believers—the church—received the Holy Spirit on the Day of Pentecost (Acts 2); we now receive the Holy Spirit at conversion. He baptizes us into the body of Christ, the church (1 Cor. 12:13). Christ has given us his Spirit as a pledge of future glory (Eph. 1:13–14).

Hendriksen writes,

The emphasis [in Rev. 22:17] is on the word *freely*. Glorious sovereign grace! This is the love of God, so touching and tender, which is addressed here to all those who have been made conscious of the need of living water. Let them not hesitate. Let them come. Let them take. It costs *them* nothing. He paid the price. So let them come, take and drink.4

The word 'freely' recalls God's promise at 21:6: 'To him who is thirsty I will give to drink without cost from the spring of the water of life.'

OBEDIENCE

We prepare for Christ's coming not only by repentance, but also by obedience to his commands. Three verses in Revelation 22 make this point:

- 'Behold, I am coming soon! Blessed is he who *keeps* the words of the prophecy of this book' (v. 7, emphasis added).
- 'I am a fellow-servant … of all who *keep* the words of this book' (v. 9, emphasis added).
- 'Behold, I am coming soon! My reward is with me, and I will give to everyone according to what he has done' (v. 12).

Obedience proves that our repentance is genuine.

The apostle Peter asks an important question: 'Since everything will be destroyed … what kind of people ought you to be? You ought to live holy and godly lives as you look forward to the day of God.' Then he writes, 'So then, dear friends, since you are looking forward to this, make every effort to be found spotless, blameless and at peace with him' (2 Peter 3:11–14).

We prepare for Christ's coming as we worship. Notice the link between obedience and worship in Revelation 22:9. John falls at the feet of an angel, who says, 'Do not do it! I am a fellow-servant with you and with your brothers the prophets and of all who keep the words of this book. Worship God!'

PRAYING

We also respond to Christ's promise, 'Yes, I am coming soon', by taking John's prayer on our lips: 'Amen. Come, Lord Jesus' (vv. 20–21). 'John's heart is filled with rapture. His soul is consumed with longing. His eye attempts to pierce the clouds. In an ecstasy of love, he exclaims, "Amen, come, Lord Jesus."'[5]

It is not easy to live the Christian life in an evil world. However, Christ gives us grace to persevere: 'The grace of the Lord Jesus be with God's people. Amen' (v. 21). The Amplified Bible defines 'God's people' as 'the saints ... (those set apart for God, to be, as it were, exclusively His)'. Christians are, even now while on earth, saints! By God's grace, we aim to live as saints, waiting for Christ's return. As God's people we are to encourage one another to perseverance: '... and let us consider how we may spur one another on towards love and good deeds. Let us not give up meeting together, as some are in the habit of doing, but let us encourage one another—and all the more as you see the Day approaching' (Heb. 10:24–25).

God's grace comes to us through 'the Lord Jesus' (v. 21), who 'is the sum, substance and glory of every vision seen by John on the island of Patmos. All that John saw and wrote ... was about the glorious and gracious work of our Lord Jesus Christ.'[6]

What is the last word in the Bible? 'Amen'—'So be it!' (v. 21). John prays for the fulfilment of Christ's promise—his coming—when he will crush his enemies and reward his saints. When he comes, will you run in terror from him or run with joy to greet him?

Notes

1 **Richard Brooks,** *The Lamb Is All the Glory: The Book of Revelation* (Welwyn Commentary; Welwyn: Evangelical Press, 1986), p. 192.
2 Ibid., p. 200.
3 Ibid.
4 **Hendriksen,** *More Than Conquerors: An Interpretation of the Book of Revelation* (London: Inter-Varsity Press, 1962), p. 210.
5 Ibid.
6 **Donald Fortner,** *Discovering Christ in Revelation* (Darlington: Evangelical Press, 2002), p. 507.

About Day One:

Day One's threefold commitment:

- To be faithful to the Bible, God's inerrant, infallible Word;
- To be relevant to our modern generation;
- To be excellent in our publication standards.

I continue to be thankful for the publications of Day One. They are biblical; they have sound theology; and they are relative to the issues at hand. The material is condensed and manageable while, at the same time, being complete—a challenging balance to find. We are happy in our ministry to make use of these excellent publications.

JOHN MACARTHUR, PASTOR-TEACHER, GRACE COMMUNITY CHURCH, CALIFORNIA

It is a great encouragement to see Day One making such excellent progress. Their publications are always biblical, accessible and attractively produced, with no compromise on quality. Long may their progress continue and increase!

JOHN BLANCHARD, AUTHOR, EVANGELIST AND APOLOGIST

Visit our web site for more information and to request a free catalogue of our books.

www.dayone.co.uk

The Gospel in Genesis
From Fig Leaves to Faith

D MARTYN LLOYD-JONES

144PP PAPERBACK, ISBN 978–1–84625–137–5

If you've ever asked, 'Why am I the way that I am? Why is life so hard? Is there any hope?' you'll find answers in Martyn Lloyd-Jones's study of Genesis.

In this series of never-before-published sermons, beloved teacher Martyn Lloyd-Jones walks readers through the early chapters of Genesis. *The Gospel in Genesis* starts with the fall of man and ends with the call of Abram as it examines portions of chapters 3–12. Along the way, Lloyd-Jones talks of serpents and sin, of the Word of God and the Babel of man. But the destination of *The Gospel in Genesis* is clear: readers will be moved from fig leaves in the garden to faith in the gospel.

Thus Lloyd-Jones preaches the gospel of Jesus Christ from the pages of Genesis. These nine sermons will snap nonbelievers out of their apathy toward God and will embolden believers to share the only gospel that offers answers to life's biggest questions.

Dr D Martyn Lloyd-Jones (1899–1981) was minister of Westminster Chapel in London for thirty years. His many books have brought profound spiritual encouragement to millions around the world. He believed that, even in a secular age, people respond to the uncompromising truth—a view which was confirmed as he saw the liberal churches emptying and the evangelicals maintaining their cause.

COLIN N PECKHAM

128PP PAPERBACK, ISBN 978–1–84625–138–2

Here is doctrine made simple! It is easy to read, necessary to grasp and thrilling to experience! Many people in our churches today do not understand the basic doctrines of salvation. In these important studies, Colin Peckham examines the great gospel words 'repentance', 'justification', 'regeneration' and 'assurance', showing how each aspect is vital in 'salvation' as a whole. Colin Peckham taught biblical doctrine for years and his expertise in making things understandable, as well as his passion for reaching the lost, are clearly seen here. His emphasis is not merely academic, but brings the challenge of an encounter with the God who made this salvation possible.

The late Revd Dr Colin Neil Peckham was born in South Africa, where he had an evangelistic ministry before entering Bible college in Cape Town. He then emigrated to Great Britain and was principal of the Faith Mission Bible College, Edinburgh, Scotland. As principal emeritus he had an extensive preaching ministry in Britain and abroad and authored several books. He was married to Mary (née Morrison) from the Isle of Lewis, Scotland. They had three adult children and two grandchildren. Colin passed away in 2009, followed some months later by Mary.

This further work from the pen of Dr Colin Peckham on 'great gospel words' is most welcome, especially at a time when the average church member has no real understanding of the essential elements of the gospel.
—*Revd Tom Shaw BA, MTh, Congregational minister, N. Ireland, and former President of the Faith Mission*

I Believe ...
The Apostles' Creed Simply Explained

TIMOTHY CROSS

128PP PAPERBACK, ISBN 978–1–84625–201–3

Christians should be well grounded in the faith 'which was once for all delivered to the saints' (Jude 3). We should know what we believe, why we believe it, and the scriptural basis for our beliefs. In this book, Timothy Cross provides a 'primer' in the key doctrines of Christianity as he explains each line of the Apostles' Creed, one of the clearest and most succinct distillations of the Christian faith ever written. Whether you are a Christian of many years' standing, a new Christian, or just interested in the Christian faith, read this book to gain a firmer grounding in the fundamentals of biblical Christianity.

Timothy Cross comes from Cardiff, Wales, and has lived in Belfast, Northern Ireland. He studied Theology at Cardiff University and then trained as an RE and Games teacher at Aberystwyth University. He is the author of over twenty Christian books and numerous articles in Christian periodicals. In 2002 he was awarded an honorary Doctor of Sacred Literature by the Christian Bible College, Rocky Mount, North Carolina, in recognition of his written ministry. Dr Cross has a preaching/Bible teaching ministry and since 1989 has broadcast a monthly Bible-based message on the South Wales Talking Magazine. His life's passions include biblical languages, distance running and the beaches of South Wales.

Timothy Cross has a passion for making truth both interesting and infectious. This exploration of the Apostles' Creed is an example of his love for the Bible and his desire to make it relevant to today's generation. I thoroughly recommend this volume.
—DR DEREK W. H. THOMAS, PROFESSOR OF THEOLOGY, REFORMED THEOLOGICAL SEMINARY, JACKSON, USA

The Sovereignty and Supremacy of King Jesus
Bowing to the Gracious Despot

MIKE ABENDROTH

240PP PAPERBACK, ISBN 978–1–84625–267–9

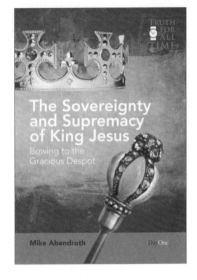

What thoughts flood our minds when we think about God? Do we think of Him as King? If so, what kind of King? In this book Mike Abendroth seeks to address a twofold problem: most Christians do not consider God as any type of Monarch, and, if they do, they think about monarchs that are weak rather than reflecting on the utter Lordship of God, the ultimate King.

In Part 1, Mike Abendroth demonstrates that the whole Bible reveals God as King. In Part 2, he describes the life-changing implications that flow from that revelation. Filled with insightful quotations, worshipful hymns, and thoughtful study questions, this book helps us to biblically embrace God as our King.

Mike Abendroth graduated from The Master's Seminary (M. Div.) in 1996 and became the pastor of Bethlehem Bible Church, West Boylston, MA, in 1997. He received his Doctorate of Ministry in Expository Preaching at the Southern Baptist Theological Seminary in 2006. One of his passions is training men to teach the Bible expositionally. He is the author of *Jesus Christ: the Prince of Preachers* (Day One, 2008). Mike is married to Kimberly and they have four children.

I wholeheartedly endorse this book and strongly encourage you to carefully read its message. Mark up its pages. Devour its truths. Share it with others. Use it as an evangelistic tool. Draw from it to preach. Use it to teach small group Bible studies. You will find this book to be an invaluable resource.
STEVEN J. LAWSON, SENIOR PASTOR, CHRIST FELLOWSHIP BAPTIST CHURCH, MOBILE, ALABAMA

IAIN D CAMPBELL

96PP PAPERBACK, ISBN 978–1–84625–082–8

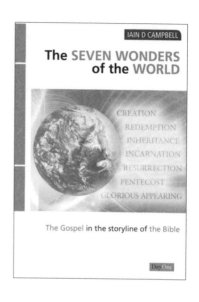

What's the big story that ties together all the little stories of the Bible? In this short book Iain D Campbell tries to answer that question by emphasizing seven key points on which the storyline of the Bible hangs. These are seven moments of awe-inspiring activity on the part of God in the history of the world, events which revolve around Jesus Christ, whom the Bible portrays as the Saviour we all need.

Revd Dr Iain D Campbell is pastor of a church on the Isle of Lewis. He trained for the ministry at the University of Glasgow and at the Free Church College Edinburgh. He is married to Anne, a teacher, and they have three children. Iain is the author of several other books published by Day One: *On the First Day of the Week*, *God, the Christian and the Sabbath*, *The Gospel According to Ruth*, *Opening Up Exodus* and *Opening Up Matthew*.

What an ideal book for a generation which is biblically illiterate, yet fascinated by stories! For Iain Campbell shows how the Bible tells the greatest of all stories—which has

moreover the merit of being true. Taken together, these seven highlights of God's saving activity provide a rounded picture of the Person in whom alone salvation is to be found—the Lord Jesus Christ. Dr Campbell has mastered the art of profound simplicity, with a wealth of teaching contained in an accessible and fascinating narrative. 'Wonderful' in more than one sense!
EDWARD DONNELLY, MINISTER, TRINITY REFORMED PRESBYTERIAN CHURCH, NEWTOWNABBEY AND PRINCIPAL, REFORMED THEOLOGICAL COLLEGE, BELFAST

JOEL JAMES

208PP PAPERBACK, ISBN 978–1–84625–269–3

How do you relate to God? Moses said to Israel, 'You shall fear the LORD your God; you shall serve Him and cling to Him ...' (Deut. 10:20). In other words, knowing God is a perfect paradox: He is both too great to approach and too great not to. When we study the God of the Bible, we should be both overwhelmed by His incomparable majesty and irresistibly drawn to His love.

In this warm and easy-to-read study of the attributes of God, Joel James captures and encourages that worshipful blend of awestruck fear and irrepressible love. Because it is built around key Old Testament 'Sunday school' stories of God's working with people such as Moses, Jonah, Ahab, and Manasseh, this book avoids the pitfalls of philosophical abstraction. It won't simply teach you who God is, it will also help you to love Him.

Joel James has an M.Div. and a D.Min. from The Master's Seminary and is the pastor-teacher of Grace Fellowship in Pretoria, South Africa. He and his wife, Ruth, have been married since 1993 and have two children.

In *Taste and See That the Lord Is Good*, Joel James has produced an intensely practical tool for the church at large. The result of his fresh angle and dynamic style is an easily comprehended introduction to the person of God. Because of the thorough expositions contained in this book, the resulting portrait of God is as deep as it is vibrant, serving as an accessible resource to anyone seeking to better understand the nature and character of God.

Dr JOHN MACARTHUR, PASTOR-TEACHER, GRACE COMMUNITY CHURCH, SUN VALLEY, CALIFORNIA